TABLE OF CONTENTS

A while back, I cleaned up and published 200 dark, crumbling songsheets housed at the Klau Library at Hebrew Union College. The librarians at the Klau had named their collection "American Yiddish Penny Songs by Morris Rund and Others," so I used the same title. The book is simply facsimiles of the original broadsides and you can get it at http://yiddishemporium.com.

Then I hunted for the melodies associated with the lyrics printed on the songsheets, and issued 39 of my favorite songs in Yiddish Songs of the Gaslight Era Volume I. Since I continued to research the era and continued to find interesting and forgotten songs, here is a second volume. There are no songs written to English / American melodies here, these songs were as originally written for Yiddish-speaking audiences.

The early twentieth century was a heyday for Yiddish theater in New York. Not only were there hundreds of productions being staged and hundreds of songs being written for the Yiddish operettas and musicals -- there were Yiddish "variety shows" and vaudeville productions. Pianos were advertised in the newspapers every day as being essential to a respectable household.

My selections avoid the most sexist, racist material, but the overweening misogyny of the period is very much in evidence. Also in evidence: folk wisdom, topical humor, historical events as seen while they unfolded. I hope this material can serve as a primary source for researchers looking to animate the world of the early twentieth century Lower East Side.

Also of interest, I hope, is the Germanic (Daytshmerish) Yiddish of the time, the exuberant use of English, often shoehorned into Yiddish grammar, and transliterations a Yiddishist of today, schooled in the YIVO standards, will shudder at.

There is more information about all these songs on the companion blog, yiddishpennysongs.com (search by song title) - and I have also posted most of the songs on youtube. Feel free to write me if you have questions -- or corrections!

Jane Peppler
jane@mappamundi.com

There are two companion cds, *Der East Side fun amol* and *Vos hot men tsu mir?* available, along with Volume 1 of the Gaslight series, *Yiddish Songs from Warsaw* and many other Yiddish songbooks, tunebooks, books, and cds, at

YiddishEmporium.com

Af a shteyndl

Translated into Yiddish by/for Natania Davrath

Russian folk melody

Af a shteyndl zits ikh mir un a hekl halt ikh mir

S'iz a hak in hand bay mir shnits a shtek in a tsam far dir

Un a gortn flants ikh, mit a flor farzets ikh

Ver es hobn nit farflantstn kroyt iz mayn gortn fartik greyt

Mit a shpan iz kum arayn lomir beyde gertners zayn

I sit on a stone and hold an axe
It's an axe in my hand, I whittle a stick into a fence for you
And I plant a garden, I plant it with a flower
Whoever hasn't planted cabbage: my garden is ready
Come in with a bucket, let's both be gardeners

The Russian
I sit on a stone and hold an axe
There's an axe in my hand, I whittle a stick into a fence for you
And I plant a garden, I plant it with a flower
Whoever hasn't planted cabbage: my garden is ready
Come in with a bucket, let's both be gardeners

Я на камушке сижу,
Я топор в руках держу

Я топор в руках держу.
Вот я колышки тешу.

Вот я колышки тешу,
Изгород горожу,

Изгород горожу,
Я капусту сажу,

Я капусту сажу
Да все беленькую

Да все беленькую,
Я кочаненькую,

У кого нету капусты,
Прошу к нам в огород.

Прошу к нам в огород,
Во девичий хоровод.

אויף יענער זייט

פֿון י. גאָרדין'ס
"טהרת המשפחה"

AUF JENER SEIT

WORDS & MUSIC
BY S. MOGULESCO.

SUNG BY
MISS JENNIE GOLDSTEIN.

PUBLISHED BY
A. GOLDBERG
398 GRAND ST, N.Y.

PIANO 50 c.

VIOLIN 30 c.

AUF JENER SEIT.

Introd.

By S. MOGULESKO.

Der mentch schtreibt nor zu wer - en reich er wen-tan die schlechste sach ___ Er schwin-delt reist die Haüt fin eich, a bi nor zu kreigen gelt a sach Nor pliz im kimt a- rous der sod der chu-chim wert gur bank - rupt ___ In keite lech firt men im ganz weit in prison fin je - ner seit, fin je-ner seit, fin je-ner seit; Weil

6

REFRAIN.

Man strives only to become rich, he turns to doing wicked things
He swindles, tears the skin from you just to get a lot of money
But suddenly the secret comes out: the "wise" fellow goes bankrupt.
They carry him off in chains, far away, in prison, on the other side

Because you, little man, are never sated.
You rob poor people just for money.
You think you'll live forever, you fool, but you'll get your punishment for it
In the grave, there on the other side

ALTS FAR GELT

Here are two versions of the song. Aaron Lebedeff copyrighted his version. Henri Gerro, a coupletist who made his career in France, later wrote his own version.

Far gelt vet aykh libn a yeder
Far gelt halt men eytses mit aykh
Far gelt krigt ir koved keseyder
Far gelt tsit men di hitel far aykh
Far gelt zayt ir bay yedn tayer
Far gelt hot aykh yederer lib
Far gelt vet men loyfn in fayer
Un far gelt iz afile in grib

Alts far gelt nor far gelt, dos bisele mezumen
Alts far gelt un nor far gelt kent ir alts bakumen
S'iz keyn zakh ikh shver far aykh
Ven ir hot gelt un ir zent raykh
Oy vayl dos gantse velt hot lib dos bisl gelt

Far gelt vert ir fun mies sheyn
Far gelt vert ir fun narish klug
Far gelt hot ir bay yedn kheyn
Far gelt hot ir seykhl genug
Far gelt hot ir sheyne karetn
Far gelt lebt ir zikh zeyer sheyn
Far gelt est ir gute kotletn
Un far gelt trinkt ir dem bestn vayn

Far gelt oykh an altitshke dame
Far gelt krigt zi a yungitshkn fraynt
Far gelt zogt er ir ketsele, mame,
Far gelt kusht der bokher ir hant
Far gelt makht er ir komplimentn
Far gelt hot zi bay im oykh a vert
Far gelt koyft er ir oykh prezentn
Nor on gelt shikt er zi tif in dr'erd

*Because of money everybody will love you
Because of money people ask your advice
Because of money you always are respected
Because of money people tip their hats
to you Because of money you're dear to
everyone Because of money everybody loves
you For money you'll run into fire And for
money, you'll run even into the grave*

*Everything for money, only money, the little
bit of cash... Everything for money, it's only
money that'll get you everything. I swear to
you, there's nothing to it, if you have money
and you're rich Yikes, the whole world loves
the little bit of money.*

*With money, if you're ugly you become
beautiful With money, if you're stupid
you become clever With money, you have
charm for everyone With money, you have
enough wisdom With money, you have
lovely carriages With money, you live very
beautifully With money, you eat good cutlets
And with money you drink the best wine*

*Because of money, an old lady Because of
money, she procures a young friend Because
of money he calls her kitten, mama, Because
of money he kisses her hand Because
of money he compliments her Because
of money she's valuable to him Because
of money he buys her presents, too, But
without money he sends her to the devil.*

NOV 22 1923

AARON LEBEDEFF
60 Second Avenue
NEW YORK

Words & music
By Aaron Lebedeff

Alts far gelt

Aaron Lebedeff 1923

Here is the Henri Gerro version:

Ikh hob far a teme genimen
A zakh velkhe hersht af der velt
Far velkher me ken alts bakimen
a zakh vemens nomen iz gelt
geyn gefin pieniądze, matbeye
kesef, yes, money, l'argent
ver s'hot es bay dem iz di deye
A koyekh in gelt iz faran

alts far gelt alts far gelt
a bisele mezimen
alts far gelt alts far gelt
ken men alts bakimen
es iz keyn zakh ikh shver bay aykh
ven ir hot gelt un ir zent raykh
vayl af gelt nor shtelt di gantse velt

far gelt koyft men op dem gevisn
far gelt yeder gornisht vert groys
far gelt zitsn mentshn in tfise
far gelt lozt men merder aroys
far gelt shteyt a khazn baym omed
far gelt vartn shayles der rov
far gelt shvert men libe af tomed
far gelt vert fun libe a sof

far gelt vern mentshn gazlonim
far gelt hot men lib un oykh faynt
far gelt gute fraynd vern soynim
far gelt vert fun soyne a fraynt
far gelt makh men zikh far a goylem
far gelt iz men feik af mord
far gelt afile oyfn beys oylem
farkimt men a besern ort

far gelt koyft a kale a khosn
far gelt iz men moykhl a khet
far gelt vert a shidekh geshlosn
far gelt oykh bakimt men a get
far gelt vern froyen shatinkes (chestnut)
far gelt vern froyen blondin
far gelt vern zey oykh brunetkes
far gelt vert a man gel un grin

I've taken as my theme
something which rules the world,
For which you can get everything:
a thing called money.
Go find money, cash,
money, money, money
One who has it has the influence!
There is strength in money.

Everything for money, a little dough
Everything for money, for money you get everything
It's nothing, I swear to you,
twhen you have money and you're rich
Because money makes the world go round

For money you sell your conscience
For money you love and also hate.
For money you go to jail,
For money they let a murderer go free.
For money a cantor sings at his stand
For money questions await the rabbi
For money one swears eternal love
For money love comes to an end

For money people become thieves
For money one loves and also hates
For money good friends become enemies
For money, enemies become friends.
For money you make a fool of yourself
For money you get good at murder
For money, even at the cemetery you get a better plot

For money a bride buys a bridegroom
For money one's sin is excused
For money a match is made.
And also, for money you get divorced.
For money women color their hair chestnut,
For money they become blondes.
For money they also become brunettes
For money a man turns a greenish yellow

12

ARAYNGEGANGEN ZIKH OYSGEDREYT UN AROYSGEGANGEN TSURIK

I took a walk once with five good friends
We passed by a big restaurant.
One of them proposed I should pay for a treat
When I went in I saw I had no money with me.

I went in, I turned around and went back out!
I changed my mind in that very blink of an eye!
As if awaking from sleep, I took to my heels.
I went in, I turned around and went back out

When Minnie sent me to find work, she went with me,
Because she knows I can't land a job on my own.
Passing by on West Broadway we saw a sign:
"A strong man needed!" Minnie says: "Well? Go in!"

I was broke! I suddenly had a thought:
"I'll become a thief, I'll rob a bank."
I decide to do it in the middle of the day.
I run into the bank with a pistol.
A policeman's standing by the door.

Arayngegangen zikh oysgedreyt

Isidore Lillian

Joseph Rumshinsky 1917

Ge

nu - men a 'walk' hob ikh a mol mit fin - f gi - te frant far - bay - ge - gan - gen

zen - en mir a groys - n res - to - rant. Un ey - ner makht a for - shlag az a

'treat' tsol - n zol ikh un vi ikh gey a - rayn, der - ze ikh, ikh

hob keyn gelt bay zikh! ikh bin a - rayn - ge - gan - gen un zikh oys - ge - dreyt un a

roys ge - gan - gen tsu - rik Ikh hob my 'mind' ge - chan - ged in dem

zelb - n oy - gn - blik. kh'hob vi fun shlof zikh oyf - ge - khapt, di

fis af di pleyt - ses a - royf - ge - brakht kh'bin a - rayn ge - gan - gen un zikh

oys - ge - dreyt un a - roys ge - gan - gen tsu - rik! rik!

Ven Min - nie shikt mir zukh - n ar - bet geyt zi mit mir mit.
vayl zi veyst az ikh a - leyn ge - vin keyn ar - bet nit. Mir
gey - en far - bay in Vest Brod - vey, der - zen hot zi a "sign." "Far -
langt a shtark - n man!" Zogt zi tsu mir: "Nu, gey a - rayn!"

Ge - ven bin ikh ge - brokh - n, krig ikh pluts - ling a ge - dank. A
gan - ef vel ikh ver - n, kh'vel ba - gan - ve - nen a bank. "In
mit - n hel - n tog zol dos ge - shen!" kler ikh bay mir. Mit a
"pis - tel" loyf ikh in der bank, shteyt a po - lits - man bay der tir!

15

Az du kenst nit un veyst nit, nemt men zikh nit unter!

Hyman Altman

Perlmutter & Wohl

A yungerman hot nit lang gebrakht fun yurop zayn vaybl do

A mol kumt er fun dem shop bay nakht, er zet zayn vaybl iz in shtub nishto

Nor plutsling kumt a shokhn tsu geyn: "Arestet hot men zi in gas!"

Der man loyft shnel vi er hot zi nor gezen, dan vert er beyz un zogt tsu ir mit kas:

An alter man mit groye hor er shmekt shoyn af yener velt

Er nemt a meydl fun akhstn yor zi heyrat mit im vayl er hot fil gelt

Itst plogt zi im un zogt im gor prost: "Ikh vil du zolst mikh geyen getn glaykh."

"S'taytsh, host mikh mayn gants gelt upkekost!" Dan vert zi kalt un entfert mit a lakh:

This is a worldwide rule everybody knows:
As soon as one has a bit of money he must become proficient.
My landsman earned a lot of money, he soon went into business with somebody
And now he comes to me crying and lamenting.
I answer him: It has to be this way

Don't go where you don't belong, it'll be healthier for you.
If you don't have the ability or the understanding, don't undertake it.
If you can't manage it and you don't understand it - don't try it.

A young man brought his wife over from Europe recently.
One night he came home from the shop, he sees his wife isn't at home.
Suddenly a neighbor comes: "They arrested her in the street!"
The man runs quickly and when he sees her he angrily says to her:

Don't go where you don't belong, it'll be healthier for you.
If you don't have the ability or the understanding, don't undertake it.
If you can't manage it and you don't understand it - don't try it.

An old man with grey hair, already smelling like the world to come,
He takes an 18-year-old girl. She marries him because he's loaded.
Now she complains to him and says bluntly: "Give me a divorce right now!"
"What?! You cost me all my money!" She coldly answers with a laugh:

Don't go where you don't belong, it'll be healthier for you.
If you don't have the ability or the understanding, don't undertake it.
If you can't manage it and you don't understand it - don't try it.

אזא מזל אויפ'ן קייזער

גענוגגען פון ה' סאמועל ראזענשטיין

אין פיפעל'ס טהעאטער	געלעבט און געלאבט	אין מ. גאלדבערגס ניע פיעסע

"LIVE and LAUGH"

ליריקס פון

ה' איזידאר ליליען

מוזיק פון

ה' הערמאן וואהל

ה' איזידאר ליליען

ה' סאמועל ראזענשטיין אלס דזשוליום

Published by WILLIAM PASTERNAK, New York.

Aza mazl afn kayser

Isidor Lillian

Herman Wohl 1918

Aza mazl auf'n Keiser

Imer flegn mentshn zikh baklogn:
Hot men eynem ongekhapt in strit,
Gefregt im "how is biznes," flegt er zogn:
"Groyse tsores, biznes toygn nit."
Git atsind a freg a biznesman: vi geyt di biznes, mister?"
Fregt dem butsher, fregt dem grocer, fregt dem shnayder,
fregt dem shuster.
Veln zey zikh nit baklogn, zikh nit ampern, nit shlogn,
Tsuzamen, on reklamen, veln zey aykh zogn:

Aza mazl afn kayser, asa mazl afn kayser...
Fregt a fraynd "Vi geyt es aykh?"
Dan entfert er aykh glaykh:
Aza mazl afn kayser, aza mazl afn kayser.
Zol der beyzer, daytsher kayser in di hayzer geyn.

Charlie iz geven a tsaytungs shrayger,
A signalman, gezunt vi a soldat,
Geshribn nor az er hot faynt di vayber,
Biz er hot gor khasene gehat.
Host geheyrat, zog ikh, Charlie,
tkumt dokh dikh tsu gratulirn.
Bistu gliklekh? Zog keyn lign, entfert er mikh mit a nign:
Mayn fraynd, you know, vos far a froy ikh hob gekrign...

Aza mazl afn kayser, asa mazl afn kayser...
Es iz a veytik tsu mayn layb, oy, gevald, hob ikh a vayb!
Aza mazl afn kayser, asa mazl afn kayser...
Zi heyst Sore, aza tsore, af dem kayser nor.

Uncle Sam iz yetst in der milkhome
Yeder birger nemt di shverd in hand,
Fun dem daytshn hund nemen nekome,
Kempfn far dem frayen foterland.
Oysgefunen hot der daytsh, di Yenkee boys kenen shlogn
Itst halt er in eyn antloyfn un zey haltn in eyn yogn
Heldish kempft oykh dort a yidl, halt a biks onshtot a nidl,
Er shist fun trentsh un zingt in "French" dos zelbe lidl:

Aza mazl afn kayser, asa mazl afn kayser...
Shisn froyen, alte layt,
Dos ken der daytsh, der khvat.
Aza mazl afn kayser, asa mazl afn kayser...
Men vet di daytshn gut tsupatshn
Un martshn keyn Berlin.

People always used to complain, when you caught up with them in the street, you asked a guy: "How's business," he'd say: "Blegh, it's lousy." Now if you ask a businessman, "how's it going, mister?" -Ask the butcher, the grocer, the tailor, the shoemaker -They won't complain, they won't answer, they won't hit you, Together, without broadcasting it, they'll say to you:

"The Kaiser should have my luck." Ask a friend, "How's it going?", He'll say the same thing. "I wish my luck on the Kaiser!" May that evil German Kaiser go begging around the village."

Charlie wrote for the newspapers. A single man, healthy as a soldier. He wrote that he hated women, (that is, until he got married). I go walking on Second Avenue, I meet up with Charlie, he's walking, too. "You got married, Charlie!" I say, "I've come to congratulate you!" "Are you happy? Don't lie." He answers with a tune. "My friend, you know what kind of a wife I got!"

"The Kaiser should have my luck! It's a misery in my life, oy gevald, what a wife I have!" "May the Kaiser have luck like this. Her name's Sore, she's a misery - if only the Kaiser had her!"

Uncle Sam's in the war now. Every citizen's taking a sword in hand, Getting revenge on the German dog, Fighting for the free Fatherland. The German found out the Yankee boys can fight. Now he's always running and they're always rushing after him. The Jew's also fighting heroically, holding a rifle instead of a needle. He shoots from the trench and sings in French this same song:

"The Kaiser should have this luck! The jaunty fellow shoots women and old people. This luck on the Kaiser: the Germans will be beaten up and we'll march to Berlin."

DIE BLVMEN KRENZE

דיא

כלומען קרענצע

PIANO
50

VIOLIN
30

WORDS AND MUSIC
BY
SOLOMON SMALL

PUBLISHED BY

THEODORE LOHR

286 GRAND ST., NEW YORK

Der blumenkrants

Solomon Small (Smulewitz)
1911

It's a wedding, people are milling about
There's no lack of carriages or inlaws
Musicians are playing. Well dressed dandies,
They're dancing with the pretty young ladies.
And the bridegroom shines from happiness
The bride so pretty in her wedding dress
Friends from everywhere make a circle around them
With a loving glance wishing them every happiness
Then there's a parade, bridegroom and bride's side!

Then they're given a wreath of flowers
And there's a fine dance.
The flowers smell good. But... can it be?
The bridegroom and bride feel sadness and pain
The garland of flowers doesn't bloom long
Happiness only knows how to run away,
The shine is gone, the dance is over,
Only twigs remain from the wreath of flowers.

Death played out its game.
Many carriages and coaches are coming.
A man died here,
One who'd done a lot of good.
One who was known as a scholar,
one who was esteemed highly.
People are coming to pay their last respects today.
Many friends have gathered.
They give charity and go to the cemetery.
The separation is so hard, and a tear falls
He's become a ghost, they make an eyl mole for him.

One leaves a garland of flowers by the grave
Because this is his last dance.
So let there be pomp, he lies in the earth,
Everyone's heart feels sadness and pain.
The garland of flowers doesn't bloom long,
Happiness only knows how to fly away.
The shine is gone, the dance is over,
Only twigs remain from the garland of flowers.

Chicken

Copyright Rubin Doctor January 1922

Ikh veys fun a gu-ter zakh vos iz gut far a-le glaykh chick-en oy oy oy chick-en

Geyt af a sim-khe af a bris est nor nit keynfleysh keyn fish chick-en

oy oy oy chick-en Keyn mol vet ir zikh ba-klog-n dreyen vet aykh keyn

mol der mog-n un baym harts-n vet aykh keyn mol drik-n Li-be ment-shn

folgt mayn plan vilt ir zayn ge-zunt un fine, est chick-en oy oy oy chick-en

Chick-en oy oy oy chick-en du bist a may-khl

dos vet aykh der-kvik-n a pul-ke a fis a shti-kl bey-lek s'iz ge-shmak a

ye-der khey-lik chick-en oy oy oy chick-en oy oy oy chick-en

Meydlekh zaynen ikh bakant, az me ruft zey do in landt
Chicken, oy oy oy chicken
Yeder 'hall' in yeder 'stoop' kukt oys vi a chicken coop
Mit chicken, oy oy oy chicken
Eyn alte moyd fun fertsik yorn dar un mies un opgeforn
Paint un powder in ale zibn glikn
Catcht arayn a grinem yung un rat im az zi iz a spring -
chicken, oy oy oy chicken

This tune appears in the Itzik Zhelonik "Yiddish Songs of Warsaw" collection with a parodic lyric, Meydlekh sheyne meydlekh.

Henry Sapoznik wrote another verse and a rhyming translation (see below):

A chicken's lebn iz nit gring
Vest yetst lernen yedersding
Fin chickens, oy nebekh, chicken
Tsi der shoykhet in di fri
Vert es bald a fricasee
Fin chickens, a top mit chickens
Trakht itst fin di kinder zeyer
Yusemlakh, di pitsl eyer
Di mame ligt shoyen ergets mit a meyer.
Libe mentshn her zikh tsu,
Loz zey lebn, est tofu
Nit chickens, oy est nit chickens.

REFREN

Chickens, oy est nit chickens
Tsum oylem habo zolst di zey nit shikn.
Hot rakhmones af der feygl,
Loz es lebn, est a beygl.

Ich vase fun n ᵬitter zach,
Vus is git far alle glach,
Chicken, oi, oi, oi, Chicken
Gait off a stmcha, off a BRISS
Ast nor nit kine flaish, kine fis,
        nor Chicken, oi, oi, oi, Chicken
Kine mul vat enr sich barklugen,
Drsen vat ich kine muhl der mugen,
In bam hertzen vat ich kine mohl dricken,
Leibe manschen falgt mein plan,
Velt ear zine gezind in fine,
Ast Chicken, oi, oi, oi, Chicken

Chicken, oi, oi, oi Chicken,
Sis a machel, dus vat ich erkvicken,
Apulke, a fees, a schtickel bailek,
Sis geschmarck a yeder cailick,
Chicken, oi, oi, oi, Chicken.

                2.
Maidlich zannen ich becannt,
A me reeft zeh du in landt,
Chicken, oi, oi, oi Chicken,
Yeder hall in yeder stoop,
Keekt aus vee a chicken coup,
Mit chicken, oi, oi,oi, Chicken,
Ein alte moidt, fun fertzig yohren,
Dar, in mees, in upgeforen,
Paint in powder, in alle zibben'glicke
Catcht a rine a greenem ying,
In rat im an zee is a Spring,
Chicken, oi, oi, oi, Chicken.

        Chorus (repeat same chorus)

I know a good thing, it's good for everyone: chicken. Go to a celebration, a bris, don't eat meat or fish, just chicken. You'll never complain, it won't knot up your stomach, it won't give you heartburn. Dear people, obey my plan, you'll be happy and healthy: eat chicken. Chicken, it's a dish that will delight you. A thigh, a leg, a bit of the breast, every part is delicious. Chicken.

I know girls, here in American they call them chicks. Every hall and every stoop looks like a chicken coop. With chicken. An old maid, 40 years old, skinny and ugly and shabby With makeup and powder and everything else, She catches a young guy newly arrived here and tells him she's a spring chicken.

A chicken's life is not so great. Allow me to elaborate on chickens, yes I mean chickens. To the butcher before three, by evening it's a friscassee of Chickens, a pot of chickens. Now think about the eggs they've laid there, orphans all, no one to care, their mother's with a carrot laying somewhere. Hear now what I say to you: Don't eat chickens, eat tofu! Not chickens oh please not chickens. Chickens, it's time for a change. Don't send them to their heavenly free range. For your health a chicken's great, but for a chicken it's too late. That's chickens I do mean chickens. Be a mentsh and don't finagle. Don't eat chickens, have a bagel!

THE TREMENDOUS SUCCESS OF THE "PEOPLES' THEATRE"

יענקי-דודל

דער אידישער

THE JEWISH YANKEE DOODLE

1. COMPANY.
2. BUSINESS BEFORE PLEASURE.
3. DER YIDISHER YANKEE=DOODLE.

WORDS AND MUSIC

PIANO ·50·   VIOLIN ·30·

LOUIS TERR, DEL.

MUSICAL COMEDY
~ BY ~
B. THOMASHEFSKY.

COPYRIGHTED 1905.
INTERNATION. COPYRIGHT SECURED

PERMISSION TO RENDER THEM BEFORE
AN AUDIENCE MUST BE OBTAINED FROM
THE PEOPLES THEATRE CO.

PUBLISHED BY
A. GOLDBERG,
398 GRAND ST.,
NEW-YORK

~ BY ~
LOUIS FRIEDSEL

Company (Kompani)

Isidore Lillian

Em   Am   B⁷

A - meri - ca iz a gold - en land dos get a ye - der
A mey - dl flegt a - rum - geyn mit a boy fun Ave - nue
Tsu zayn a border - ke bay a mis - ses var ikh shoyn ge -

5   Em   Am/C   Am   B⁷

tsi. Mit shvind - lers fey - kers blo - fers a - les heyst dos "Com - pa - ny" A
C. Far yed - n flegt zi ri - men zikh "Well, I keep com - pa - ny." Ge
shtroft. Lang hob ikh dort nit ge - voynt, kh'hob bald a - roys - ge - muft. Nit

10   Am   D   C   Em

gri - ner kumt a - her un makht zikh uf a "so - da stend" Dem
keept hot er ir com - pa - ny biz, hert aykh nor tsu git: Er
vayl dos es - n oder di loz - shi var dort nit git, nor

14   C   E♭ᵒ   F♯ᵒ   Eᵒ   B♭ᵒ   B⁷

tsvey - tn tog ruft er zikh shoyn Khay - im Ye - khez - kel end...
iz fun ir ant - lof - n un zi iz ge - blib - n mit...
vayl kh'hob oys - ge - fu - nen az ge - voynt hob ikh dort mit...

18   Em   Am   D   Em

Com - pa - ny Com - pa - ny Khotsh der stend ba - treft veys ikh
Zi far - shtelt zikh yetst di yor, far
Es zol gor - nit zayn oys - ge - redt, ge -

24   C   B   Em   F♯ᵒ Eᵇᵒ

nit zeyer fil dokh ruft er zikh a Com - pa - ny Com - pa -
tso - res iz zi ge - shvol - n gor...
fu - nen hob ikh in mayn bet a

29   Aᵒ Cᵒ D   Em   /G   B⁷   Em

ny Nu, ikh veys dokh a - les heyst dokh Com - pa - ny
i - mer mer vert ir shver di Com - pa - ny
Um - ge - zikht ikh ze es krikht oy Com - pa - ny

America is a golden land, as everyone admits,
With swindlers, fakers, bluffers
All known there as "company."
A greenhorn comes over and opens a soda stand,
The second day already he calls it
"Chaim Chaskel and Company"
Though the stand doesn't
Amount to very much, he still calls it a company,
So you see, everything's a company!

A girl used to go around with a boy from Avenue C,
She told everyone that they were "keeping company"
He kept her company until this became only too clear,
Then he ran off, and she was left with
Company. Now she curses the day.
Her troubles have made her swell up
And her company is growing heavier and heavier to bear.

I became a boarder in a woman's house.
But I didn't stay long; pretty soon I had to leave.
Not because the food or the room was bad
Only because I discovered that I was living there with
Company. Just don't spread this around:
In my bed I found company!
I looked around, and my crawling company was everywhere.

NATIONAL : THEATRE

HOUSTON ST. & SECOND AVE., N. Y.　　　　M. SAKS & L. GOLDBERG, Mgrs.

PERETZ SANDLER'S *Great Musical Comedy Success*

Lyrics by

Louis Gilrod

Perez Sandler

Music by

Peretz Sandler

In 3 Acts by Mr. Kalmanowitz　**PAPPA'S BOY**　אין 3 אקטען פון ה. קאלמאנאוויטש

2

גרויסע סוקסעס
לידער

ס'איז
א
קורצער
וועג

דעם

טאָטענ'ס
זיהנדעל

2

גרויסע סוקסעס
לידער

עס געהט
ווי
געשמירט

Now Playing at the **NATIONAL THEATRE** Houston St. & 2nd Ave.

PRICE 50 CENTS

TRIO PRESS, Inc., 28-30 East 4th Street, N. Y. C.

Es Geiht Vie Geshmirt

Words by
LOUIS GILROD

Music by
PERETZ SANDLER

Der mentsh er darf keynmol dokh nit blaybn shteyn
di oygn tsum himl arof
Az voyl iz tsu dem nor vos helft zikh aleyn
un nemt nit fun tsveytn keyn blof
Ven mayn kales tate ot der shtoltser gevir
derhert az zayn kind iz farfirt un ruinirt
yetst vet er kumen zikh betn bay mir
un der shidekh vet geyn vi geshmirt
men darf nor zayn a man un krign dem rikhtikn plan

Dan geyt, dan geyt vi geshmirt (2x)
Mayn Beatrice's foter er iz nokh nit poter
Zol er yetst visn ot der pipernoter
Es geyt es geyt vi geshmirt (2x)
Ikh vil im shoyn tsugreytn er zol mikh nokh betn
Es geyt es geyt vi geshmirt

"Farvos hobn mikh ale meydlekh nor faynt?"
Klogt zikh far mir haynt a boy
Er bet mikh an eytse, vi a guter fraynd
Un kh'hob im gezogt dan azoy:
A meydl hot faynt ven a boy iz tsu "slow"
Un shteyt nor baym stoop dort, dan ?
Di hayntike maydlekh libn, "you know"
A boychick mit pep un mit "juice"
Me git zey tsum tansn, a "catch"
A kush un a glet un a kvetsh

Dan geyt, dan geyt vi geshmirt (2x)
Rusishe, Daytshkes, afile Litvatshkes,
Zey loyfn shoyn nokh dan azoy vi di katshkes
Es geyt es geyt vi geshmirt (2x)
A 'voink' mit di oygn, zey kumen tsufloygn -
Es geyt es geyt vi geshmirt

A man should never just stand with his eyes on heaven The smart money's on the one who helps himself And doesn't get bluffed by anybody When my bride's father, that proud rich man, Hears that his child is seduced and ruined Now he'll come begging to me and the match will go forward as if greased You just have to be a man and have the right plan

It goes the way it's greased. My Beatrice's father isn't free yet May he now know about the monster/ nonsense It goes the way it's greased I'll prepare him so he'll beg me It goes the way it's greased

"Why do all the girls hate me?" a boy complains to me today He asks my advice as a good friend, and I told him this: A girl hates it when a boy is too slow And just stands by the stoop there Girls thesse days love, you now, A boy with pep and "juice" You get them to dance, a "catch" A kiss and a caress and a squeeze

Then it goes as if greased Russians, Germans, even Litvaks, They run after that sort of guy like ducks It goes the way it's greased A wink of your eye, they get dreamy It goes as it's greased.

אֵלוּ וְאֵלוּ צוֹעֲקִים בָּךְ

I

בעלי־בתים היושבים בבתיהם
ושותים יין בכליהם.
אלו ואלו צועקים בך:
א טרונק בראנפען ווילט זיך דאָך!

II

בעלי־בתים, וואָס וואוינען אין אייגענע הײַ
טרינקען אויס בראנפען גאַנצע ברייזער.
אלו ואלו צועקים בקול:
א טרונק בראַנפען איז דאָך וואויל!

III

דינים היושבים אצל הכנס'ל,
השותים יין א פולע פלעשעל.
אלו ואלו צועקים בקול:
אַ טרונק בראַנפען איז דאָך וואויל!

33

Eylu v'eylu

From Menakhem Kipnis 140 folkslider

Ba - le - ba - tim he - yoysh - vim   be - bo - sey - hem   v - shoy - shim   ya - yin

be - ke - ley - hem   Ey - lu vo - ey - lu tso - ya - kim bokh   a trunk bron - fn   vilt zikh dokh

Balebatim vos voynen in eygene hayzer
Trinken oys bronfn gantse brayzer
Eylu voeylu tsoyakim bekoyl, a trunk bronfn iz dokh voyl

Dayonim hayoyshvim eytsel haknesl
Hashoysim yayin fule fleshl
Eylu voeylu tsoyakim bekoyl, a trunk bronfn iz dokh voyl!

Rabonim vos lernen mishnayes peysek
Trinken bronfn mit groys kheyshek
Eylu voeylu tsoyakim bokh, a trunk bronfn vilt zikh dokh

Ganovim hayoyshvim bemakteres
Vshoysim yayin bikley kheres
Eylu voeylu tsoyakim khay, a trunk bronfn podavay!

Ganovim, vos brekhn shleser fun shtol
Trinken bronfn gor on a tsol
Eylu voeylum tsoyakim khay, a trunk bronfn podavay!

Doktoyrim vos makhn dem khoyle kranker
Trinken bronfn a gantsn anker
Eylu voeylu tsoyakim bokh, a trunk bronfn vilt zikh dokh

Hendler hayoyshvim eytsel hahendl
Vshoysim yayin a fule fendl
Eylu voeylu tsoyakim bekoyl, a trunk bronfn iz dokh voyl!

Melamdim vos lernen mit kinder gemore
Trinken bronfn in der grester tsore
Eylo voeylu tsoyakim khay, a trunk bronfn podavay!

Arbeter fun fabrikn un mayster krayen
Trinken bronfn un makhn a lekhayim
Eylo voeylu tsoyakim khay, a trunk bronfn podavay!

Homeowners who sit in their houses drinking wine from their vessels, all of them yell to you: "A drink of whiskey is wanted!"

Homeowners who live in their own houses drink all the whiskey, whole breweries full. All of them yell in one voice: "A drink of whiskey is really great!"

Rabbinic judges hanging out at shul drinking a full flask of wine, all of them yell in one voice A drink of wine is really great

Rabbis who teach mishna judgements drink wine very lustily. All of them yell to you: A drink of whiskey is wanted!

Thieves hanging out in their hiding place rink wine from ceramic jugs. All of them yell "L'chayim! Give me a drink of whiskey!"

Thieves who break the stable locks drink whiskey endlessly. All of them yell "L'chayim! Give me a drink of whiskey!"

Doctors who make their patients sicker drink a whole anchor? of booze. All of them shout out: A drink of whiskey is wanted!

Merhants, sitting by their businesses, drink a full pot of wine. All of them should at the top of their voices: A drink of whiskey is really great!

The teachers who study gemorah with the children drink booze in times of greatest trouble. All of them shout out "L'chaim! Give us a drink of whiskey!"

Factory workers and master craftsmen call out, they drink booze and say l'chaim. All shout out l'chaim together: Give us a drink of whiskey!

Far Nile, Nokh Nile

Aaron Lebedeff

Di hayntike mamzeln

Ven zey viln di boyes ayngefeln

Shmirn zikh di eygelekh mit maskere afile

ay ay ay ay

Ober in der fri

Ven s'derkikt zikh tsu zey tsi

Hobn zey a ponim vi nokh nile

Un derfar zog ikh, un gegebn dos ir ba zikh

Before Neilah, after Neilah, a boy, a girl,
each of us should behave like a decent human being

In this lifetime all of us must hold ourselves accountable
And we shouldn't be too snobbish, God forbid,
Because, my dear, the wheel turns
And later one has a face [as worn out] as after Neilah
And therefore I say, and remember this well for myself:

Today's mademoiselles, when they want to please the boys
They even smear their eyes with mascara, ay ay ay
But in the morning when they take a look at themselves
They have faces [as ugly] as after Neilah
And therefore I say, and tell you

Songs from the Latest Comedydrama
Played with Great Success at the PEOPLES THEATRE.

דאס דארפס מיידעל

THE COUNTRY GIRL

COMPOSED
AND
Arranged
BY
PERLMUTER
&
WOHL

···CONTENTS···

אינהאלט פערצייבניס:

1. Dos Bissele Erd.
2. Frauen-Rechte.
3. As du kenst nit un weist nit, nemt men sich nit unter.
4. Bist mein krein, mein welt.

.1 דאם ביסעלע ערד.
.2 פרויען-רעכבע.
.3 אז דו קענסט ניט און וויסט ניט, נעהמט מען זיך ניט אונטער.
.4 ביזט מיין קריין, מיין וועלט.

HEBREW PUBLISHING CO.
83 87 CANAL ST. NEW YORK
Copyright 1911.

Piano
each
50

Violin
each
30

36

froyen rekht

Hyman Altman

Perlmutter & Wohl 1911

Fil nay - es brengt yetst a - roys di tsayt ikh denk s'iz nit a - zoy shlekht Di

vay - ber vel - n zayn glaykh mit layt zey kemp - fn tsu hob - n fil rekht Far-

shi - de - ne froy - en fun a - ler - lay ras - n ts zen - en tsi kle - rn oys

ple - ner zey loy - fn a - rum un men spitsht in di gas - n zi ma - khn a strayk mit di

me - ner Un zey shray - en pruft nor tray - en ven nit vet ir dan ba - ray - en

Folgt nor dem gu - ten plan hert nit tsu fil dem man to - mer hot ir moy - re

vet far aykh zayn shlekht koym kumt er shpet tsu geyn far - firt im bald

in di tseyn shtelt zikh groys shrayt bald oys: Leb - n zol froy - en rekht

Fil nayes brengt yetst aroys di tsayt
Ikh denk s'iz nit azoy shlekht
Di vayber veln zayn glaykh mit layt
Zey kempfen tsu hobn fil rekht
Farshidene froyen fun alerlay rasn
Tsu zenen tsu klern oys plener
Zey loyfn arum un men sptitsht in di gasn
Tsu makhn a strayk mit di mener
Un zey shrayen pruft nor trayen
Ven nit vet ir dan barayen:

Folgt nor dem gutn plan
Hert nit tsufil dem man
Tomer hot ir moyre vet far aykh zayn shlekht
Koym kumt er shpet tsu geyn
Farfirt im bald in di tseyn
Shtelt zikh groys shrayt bald oys:
Lebn zol froyen rekht

Mir veln hobn di gantse makht
Di mener haltn far fon
Mir veln kumen nokh halbe nakht
Toyt shiker aheym fun salon
Mir veln nit zayn mer farshklaft vi atsinder
Vayl dos iz far undz nit keyn maykhl
Di mener zey veln unds hobn di kinder
Mir veln zikh gletn in baykhl
Vayber, meydn, vilt ir freydn?
Hert aykh tsu vos ikh vil redn:

Elekshon tsayt ven s'vet kumen do
Vet zayn bay undz in di hend
300 kush tsu a yeder froy
Vet gebn undz der Prezident
Mir veln nit kukn tsi greser tsi klener
Vayl mir hobn gute printsipn
Mir veln nor voutn far dem vos iz shener
Un ver es vet mer intershtipn
Ofitsirn veln krapirn mit zey zoln shpatsirn

Di froyen veln polislayt zayn
Af yedn korner tsvey, dray
Ven a ganev falt in di hent arayn
Git er nor a kush, iz er fray
Eyn zakh iz nit git fun di yetstike plener
In hartsn ken undz nokh dem klemen
Koym viln mir straykn tsi fil mit di mener
Veln zey "skebs" tsu der arbet zikh nemen
Me darf probirn git shtudirn
Nor keyn muth keyn muth farlirn

There's lots of news these days, I don't think it's so bad. The women want to be equal to men, they're struggling for a lot of rights. All sorts of women from all races are thinking up plans, they're running around making speeches in the streets. They want to strike against the men and they cry out: "Just try it --If not, you'll regret it!"

Follow this good plan, don't listen too much to your husband lest you be afraid things will go badly for you. As soon as he comes home late, pop him in the teeth. Hold your head up high, cry out: Long live women's rights!

We'll have all the power, we'll keep men just for fun. We'll come home from the salon past midnight, dead drunk. We won't be slaves any more, as we are now, because we don't find that palatable at all. The men will have the kids for us, we'll pat our bellies. Women, girls, do you want to be happy? Listen to what I tell you:

When election time comes, we'll have it in our hands: 300 kisses per woman will give us the presidency. We won't care about tall or short because we have good principles -- we'll just vote for the one who's prettier and who can advance us farther. Officers will kick the bucket, they'll go walking with them.

Women will be police officers, two or three on every corner. When a thief falls into their hands, if he just gives a kiss he's free. There's one thing about the plans these days that's not so good, it aggrieves our hearts: if we strike against the men too much they'll hire scabs. We need to experiment and study carefully, but not lose heart

געוואלט דיא מאַנטענס

GWALD DI MANTENS

WORDS AND MUSIC BY

ADOLF KING

Arranged by P. LASKOWSKY

RECORDED ON

Okeh Records

SUNG BY

MORRIS GOLDSTEIN

ADOLF KING

Gevald di mantens

Adolf King

Ven der zu-mer kumt nor on un es vert zeyer heys Ven ir geyt vi oys ge putst un preg-lt zikh in shveys

Ven ir filt ir kent nit shlofn nit es-n un nit ruen zolt ir zikh a - leyn nit blofn in di man-tens zolt ir flien

Oy di man - tens gevald di man-tens in di man-tens iz a prakht, dort iz gut zay tog say nakht

A ye - der ey - ner rut oys di bey - ner bo yes mey dn me lebt in frey dn di mantens iz al - rayt rayt

40

Ven der zumer kumt nor on un es vert zeyer heys
Ven ir geyt vi oysgeton un preglt zikh in shveys
Ven ir filt ir kent nit shlofn nit esn un nit rien
Zolt ir zikh aleyn nit blofn, in di mantens zolt ir flien

Oy di mantens, gevald di mantens
In di mantens iz a prakht, dort iz gut say tog say nakht
Yeder eyner rut oys di beyner
Boyes, meydn, men lebt in freydn, di mantens iz alright

Vayblekh nemen arum di ringlekh ven zey kumen aher.
Haynt di meydlekh mit di yinglekh, far zey iz nit shver.
"Make marriages", densing, beler, yeder hot do tsayt
(tsaat)
Hot ir amol prubirt in di mantens nemen a heyrat

Oy di mantens, gevald di mantens,
in dem heyrat iz zeyer sheyn
Oy a mekhaye iz dos tsu zen
Gleklekh klingen un ale zingen
Boyes, meydn men lebt in freydn, di mantens iz alright

Mayn shokhn iz farheyrat fuftsn yor es geyt im git
Nor eyn tsore iz mit im: er hot keyn kinder nit
Er shikt zayn vayb in di mantens tsu farbesern ir gezunt
Hert a glik: tsu nayn monatn gehat hot zi a kind!

Oy di mantens, gevald di mantens, mayn shokhn iz yetst
'satisfeyt'
Er zingt dos lidl ful mit freyd
Hert a vunder fun luft hot men kinder
Boyes, meydn men lebt in freydn, di mantens iz alright

Nor eyn khesorn hot di mantens: yeder frish
On 'ekters' un 'kolekters' geyt men nit tsum tish
Haynt batkhonim un kaptsonim, klezmers alerley
Der farmer shteyt do mit a shtekn in hant un er vart af
zey...

Oy di mantens, gevald di mantens! Shteyt a latz un
taynet ayn:
"A 'star' bin ikh, lozt mikh arayn!"
Der 'farmer' vil nit hern, ikh darf nit keyn shtern
Lome, krume, toybe, shtume, di mantens iz all right

When summer comes and it gets very hot, when you go around practically undressed and fry in your sweat, when you think you can't sleep, eat, or rest, don't fool yourself: Fly to the mountains!

Oh, the mountains, wow! In the mountains it's beautiful, it's good there day and night. Everybody rests their bones. Boys, girls, you live happily, the mountains are all right!

Wives turn their rings around when they come here. And for the girls and boys, it's not hard at all. Make marriages, dancing, balls, everybody has time here. Give it a try, maybe you'll get married in the mountains.

Oh, the mountains, wow! Getting married is a pretty thing. It's a miracle to see. Bells ringing, everybody singing. Boys, girls, you live happily, the mountains are all right!

My neighbor's been married fifteen years, it's gone well for him, he has only one sorrow: he has no children. He sent his wife to the mountains to improve her health. Hear his good fortune: in nine months, she had a child!

Oh, the mountains, wow! Now my neighbor is satisfied. He sings this song happily. Amazing! One can have children from the air itself! Boys, girls, one lives happily, the mountains are all right!

The mountains have just one drawback: at breakfast every morning you can't escape the actors and collectors. And further: jesters, paupers, all kinds of musicians. The farmer stands with a stick in his hand waiting for them.

Oh, the mountains, wow! A buffoon is complaining: "I'm a star! Leave me alone!" The farmer won't listen. "I don't need any stars." Crippled? Hunchbacked? Deaf? Mute? The mountains are all right!

GOTTENIU GIB A DREH DUS REDELE

גאָטעניו
גיב אַ דרעה
דאָס רעדעלע

From Max Gabel play "A GIRL'S REVENGE", produced at Peoples Theatre, N. Y.
Words by S. Gilrod—Music by J. M. Rumshinsky. Song featured by little Henrietta Jacobson.

CATALOGUE OF
CELEBRATED JEWISH MUSIC
FOR PIANO WITH WORDS,

PROGRAM

רייב האָרצער. אַ רייכער פאַולטרי הענדלער
מר. מאָס נעבער
טעם זיין עלטסטער זוהן. מר. וויליאם עפשטיין
אלעקס. זיין אינגסטער זוהן.
מיס רושעני גאָרדשטיין
בעני. זיין טאָכטער. מאָר. פערקוף
ראי טראָמבע. איהר מאָן. מר. דייוויד גראַ
באָבי. זייער קינד. מאסטער לובריצקי
רינא פערדמאַן. א הויז האַלטערין
מאָר. סאבינא ראָהסער
לולו. א קינד. א יתומה.
מיס העגרעטא דושיייקאָבסאָן
ישראל מאיר. הארצעריב ברודער.
מר. דושיייקאָב וועקסלער
מינא גאָרדע. זיין ווייב. מאָר. שר
רעי. א טייסרייטערקע. מיס פירלער
דושייקאָב לאנדאו. א דעטעקטיוו.
מר. יואיס נאָרר
עני. זיין טאָכטער. מיס פראָנסים פינקאָף
מר. פערקויף
זרה. אן אלטער מאָן.
מר. גאָרדשטיין
נעסט, סאָפאראדושעטאקטס. אידען אא ז וו.

Andante cantabile. (in a singing style.)   Schubert's Celebrated Serenade. Price 20¢ net.   Simplified and arr. by ALBERT TERES.

Copyright, 1908, by A. Teres, N.Y.

PUBLISHED BY A. TERES
Music Dealer and Publisher
88 DELANCEY STREET   NEW YORK

Gotenyu, gib a drey dos redele

Louis Gilrod

Joseph Rumshisky 1916

Fun tsvey - tn hoyz dos mey - de - le   trogt a naye sheyn kley - de - le   nay - e shikh un ze - ke - lekh   hot shey - ne roy - te be - ke - lekh   tseyn - de - lekh vi pe - re - lekh   sheyn far - kemp - te he - re - lekh   ir ta - te ma - me   ze - nen raykh un koy - fn ir a ye - de zakh.   Ikh hob a ta - te oykh ge - hat a mol.   Yetst bin ikh a ye - soy - me   un men plogt mikh gor on tsol!

Go - te - nyu gib a drey dos re - de - le   un helf a ye - soy - me an or - em mey - de - le   un s'khis fun mayn toy - tn ta - te - nyu   helf mayn o - rem ma - me - nyu   ta - te - nyu, bi - ter iz mir   on   dir di kin - der in gas, zey var - fn zikh mit mir.   Got, Got, may - ne tre - re - lekh der - ze un gib shoyn dos re - de - le   a drey, oy Got!

Fun tsveytn hoyz dos meydele trogt a naye sheyn kleydele
Naye shikh un zekelekh, hot sheyne royte bekelekh,
Tseyndelekh vi perelekh, sheyn farkempte herelekh.
Ir tate mame zenen raykh un koyfn ir a yede zakh.
Ikh hob a tate oykh gehat a mol.
Yetst bin ikh a yesoyme un men plogt mikh gor on tsol!

Gotenyu gib a drey dos redele un helf a yesoyme an orem meydele
Un s'khis fun mayn toytn tatenyu helf mayn orem mamenyu
Tatenyu, biter iz mir on dir
Di kinder in gas, zey varfn zikh mit mir.
Got, Got, mayne trerelekh derze un gib shoyn dos redele a drey, oy Got!

Ikh bin oykh a meydele, ikh darf oykh a sheyn kleydele!
Tsu vos kumt mir di shmates nor, kleydelekh mit lates gor?
Tut on mir zakhn reyninke, vel ikh oykh zayn a sheyninke
Un zol mayn mame zayn gezint vel ikh oykh zayn a gliklekh kind!

The girl next door has a pretty new dress, new shoes, a new purse,
She has pretty red cheeks,
Teeth like pearls, pretty combed hair.
Her parents are rich and buy her everything.
I, too, once had a father.
Now I'm an orphan and I'm endlessly plagued.

God, give the wheel a turn and help an orphan, a poor girl,
May my father in heaven intercede for my poor mother.
Father, it's bitter here for me without you,
The kids in the street bully me.
God, see my tears and give the wheel a turn.

I too am a girl, I too should have a pretty dress!
Why do I get only rags, dresses full of holes?
Put clean things on me and I, too, will be pretty.
And as long as my mother is healthy,
I too will be a happy child!

די גרינע קוזינע

יאנקעלע בריסקער

DIE GREENE KUSINE

Words by

YANKELE BRISKER

Melody Adapted from
JEWISH FOLK SONG

Arranged by
JACOB B. DAVIDSON

Author's Edition

Published by

J. LEISEROWITZ PUBLISHING CO.

200 Fifth Avenue   New York

"Di grine kuzine" was claimed by several composers. The sheet music says: "Words by Yankele Brisker, melody adapted from Jewish folk song." [Milken says this was a pseudonym for Jacob Leiserowitz]It also says "Ask for the original author's edition." Abe Schwartz copyrighted a version of the song, Hyman Prizant also claimed it. And capitalizing on its popularity, Morris Rund published a "companion" song, Mayn griner kusin, claiming the words and music (though the music is virtually identical to this one).

Di grine kuzine

Es iz tsu mir ge-ku-men a ku-zi-ne sheyn vi gold iz zi ge-ven, di gri-ne, di be-ke-lekh vi roy-te po-me-ran-tsn, fi-se-lekh vos bet-n zikh tsum tan - tsn tan - tsn

Es iz tsu mir gekumen a kuzine,	My cousin from the old country came over here.
Sheyn vi gold iz zi geven, di grine,	She was beautiful as gold, the "greenhorn."
Di bekelekh vi royte pomerantsn,	Her cheeks were rosy like blood oranges;
Fiselekh vos betn zikh tsum tantsn.	Her feet were just begging to dance.
Nit gegangen iz zi, nor geshprungen,	She skipped instead of walking;
Nit geredt hot zi, nor gezungen.	She sang instead of speaking.
Freylekh lustik iz geven ir mine,	Happy and merry was her demeanor.
Ot aza geven iz mayn kuzine.	Such was my cousin.
Ikh bin arayn tsu mayn nekst-dorke,	I went to the lady next door,
Vos zi hot a milineri-storke.	Who has a little millinery store.
A dzhab gekrogn hob ikh far mayn kuzine,	I got my greenhorn cousin a job there.
Az lebn zol di goldene medine!	"Long live the Golden Land!"
Avek zaynen fun demolt on shoyn yorn,	Many years have since past.
Fun mayn kuzine iz a tel gevorn.	My cousin has turned into a wreck.
Peydes yorn lang hot zi geklibn,	She worked on and on for many a payday,
Biz fun ir aleyn iz nisht geblibn.	Until nothing was left of her.
Unter ire bloye sheyne oygn	Under her blue, beautiful eyes
Shvartse pasn hobn zikh fartsoygn,	Black circles have appeared.
Di bekelekh, di royte pomerantsn,	The cheeks, those rosy oranges,
Hobn zikh shoyn oysgegrint in gantsn.	Have aged and lost their greenhorn glow.
Haynt az ikh bagegn mayn kuzine	Nowadays, when I meet my cousin
Un ikh freg zi, "Vos zhe makhstu, grine?"	And I ask her, "How are you, greenhorn?"
Entfert zi mir mit a krumer mine	She answers me with a scowl:
Az brenen zol Kolombuses medine!	"Columbus's land can go to hell!"

Companion Song to "DIE GREENE KOSINE"

מיין גרינער קאזין

מאטקע פוּן סלאבאטקע

MEIN GREENER KOSIN
MOTKIE fin SLOBOTKIE

Tremendous Hit!
—
SUNG AND PLAYED
ON ALL
PHONOGRAPH RECORDS
and
MUSIC ROLLS

Tremendous Hit!
—
Arranged for
PIANO
VIOLIN or MANDOLIN
With Words

WORDS and MUSIC BY

MORRIS RUND

Price 40 cents

Published By
J. & J. KAMMEN,
BROOKLYN, NEW YORK.

Mein Greener Kosin

Motkie Fin Slobotkie

Words and Music by
By MORRIS RUND
Arr. by Jack Kammen

Gekumen iz nit lang tsurik mayn griner kozin Motkie,
Gelozt hot er a vayb mit kinder dorten in Slobotkie.
Yetzt ven ir zolt zen mayn kozin, a makher, a fardiner,
Maiden krigt er af dem dozin, er brent a velt der griner.

A khasen vert mayn kozin do mit a blonde psule,
Gebobte hor, a kurze kleydl, a simkhe, a gedule.
Di khasene bashtimt shoyn Motkie,
Er nemt rooms a mekhaye,
Ver darf di grine fun Slobotkie, az er hot do a naye?

Mayn kozin hot do landslayt fil un zey vizn ale
Dort in Slobotkie hot er a vayb un do hot er a kale.
A ticket koyfn zey geshvind un shikn nokh der grine,
Gekumen iz zi mit di kinder do in der medine.

Der khupe tog hot ongerukt, mayn kozin zitst un frayt zikh.
Ver ken tsu Motken haynt zayn glaykh,
Er putzt zikh un er dreyt zikh,
Bashtelt a hol shoyn mit a khazn, es felt keyn zakh, kholile.
Haynt banakht darf geyen mayn kozin
    mekadesh zayn di psule.

Di muzik shpilt shoyn in der hol, 'siz lebedig un freylakh,
Der khasen-bokher oyben un er kukt oys vi a meylekh.
Plutzim gor, oy, hert, a vunder— es efent zikh di tiren.
Zayn vayb di grine mit di kinder brengt men im zu firn.

Opgenumen hot far shrek mayn kozin shir dos loshen.
Di grine, zi shpant glaykh arop un halt shoyn fest dem khosn.
Es vert a tuml, a behole, es kumt police tsu raytn.
Motkie khapt dort a mapole, men shlogt fun ale zaytn.

Mayn kozin iz shoyn broyn un blo, dokh eyn zakh farsheyt er:
Koym trogt er zikh nit shnel aroys blaybt er in hol a toyter.
Er khapt zayn yente fun Slobotkie antloyft vi fun a diner.
Anshtot di kale muzt gor Motkie aheym geyen mit der griner.
Anshtot di kale muzt gor Motkie aheym geyen mit der griner.

My greenhorn cousin Motkie came over recently, Left his wife and kids behind in Slobotkie. You should see him now: A big shot, loaded with money, He's got girls by the dozen. This greenhorn is going places!

Motkie gets engaged to marry a young blonde. Bobbed hair, short skirt, she's a wonder. What a joy! He sets the date, rents a fine flat. Who needs the old lady in Slobotkie when he's got a new one here!?

But my cousin has many landsmen, and they all know He's got a bride over here -- and a wife back in Slobotkie! Quickly they buy a ticket and send for his wife. She comes to America with the kids.

The wedding day arrives, Motkie is all smiles. No one can equal him today, he primps and preens. He's hired a hall, a cantor, nothing's been forgotten, God forbid. Tonight my cousin will make the young blonde his wife!

Music plays in the hall; the mood's lively and bright, The husband-to-be waits up front, looking like a king. Suddenly, listen: A wonder! The doors open ... And Motkie's wife and kids are led to his side!

My cousin is paralyzed with fear, he's mute. The greenhorn wife comes right in and clutches the bridegroom. A tumult, an uproar! The police come riding up, And Motkie meets his downfall: he's beaten up from all sides.

Soon my cousin's black and blue, but one thing he knows: If he doesn't get away fast, he's a dead man. So Motkie grabs his old lady from Slobotkie and runs away as if from thunder. He has to take his greenhorn wife home, not the new bride. He has to take his greenhorn wife home, not the new bride.

הערינג
מיט פּאטייטעס

.1

אין ניו יארק אז איהר ווילט דא א לעבען מאכען

אז איינער פעדדעלט מיט קאליבאטען זאלט איהר פון איהם ניט לאכען,

אויב איהר ווילט געהן אין ביזנעס, זאלט איהר שנעל ניט לויפען,

עפּענט אויף א סטאר און שטעלט ארויס א סיין, אין פּאנגט אן צו פערקויפען.

רעפרײן:

הערינג מיט פּאטייטעס, הערינג מיט פּאטייטעס !

א כפרה פלייש, סטייק, קאטשקע, ספּאַנדזש־קייק און טשיז־קייק !

טשיקען איז א הונד, פערגלייכענדיג צו דעם פּאַרשטעהט עס

דער בעסטער מאכל פאר דעם בייכעל — איז הערינג מיט פּאַטייטעס.

.2

עסען מענט איהר וואס איהר ווילט, עס וועט מיך ניט פאַרדריסען,

נולאש עסט דער אונגאר, גאַליציאַנער פלייש אין זיסען,

רומעניער עסען מאַ־מאַ־ליגע, גוים עסען ראָקעם

רײטשען עסען זייער־קרויט — וואָס עסען די ליטוואַקעם ?

.3

האָט ווער פון אייך א שלעכטען מאָגען און ער קען ניט קיין

האָט ווער פון אייך קיין אַפּעטיט ניט און קען ניט פערדייען

לויפט ניט צו קיין דאָקטאָר, דאָרט ליעגט ניט אייער ישועה

פאַר א שלעכטען מאָגען האָב איך דיא בעסטע רפואה.

.4

א גנב, שפּעט ביי נאַכט איז אין א הויז אַרײנגעקראָכען

דיא טירען באַלד געעפענט און דיא סייף אויפגעבראָכען

ווען ער האָט דיא סייף געעפענט איז ער שיעור אַראָב פון זינען,

געמיינט האָט ער דאָרט ליגט געלד, צום סוף האָט ער געפונען:

.5

מײן שכנה געהט צו קינד, דיא קולות געהען ביז אין סילינג

א דאָקטאָר זאָגט אז זיא האָט שוער איז פּאָזיטיוו א צווילינג

א צווייטער דאָקטאָר האָט איהר באַלד פאַר 4 קינדער געשוואָירען

ווען זיא איז געלעגען וויסט איהר וואָס זיא האָט געבוירען,

.6

אין אידישען טהעאַטער האָב איך שוין געזעהן א סך פּיעסען

דיא נעמען זיינען דיא זעלבע איך וועל זיי נישט פאַרגעסען,

דער שוואַרצער איד, דאָס פּינטעלי איד — אַלע דאָס ווייסען

פאַר וואָס זאָל א שרייבער ניט מאַכען א פּיעסע זיא זאָל הייסען,

.7

עס קומט דאָך אן עלעקשאָן, דאַן זאָלט איהר זיך ניט מישען

דעמאָקראַטען, רעפּאַבליקאַנער זאָלען זיך שלאַנגען קאָפּ אין קישען

רוזוועלט, טעפּט און מיסטער ווילסאָן, פון זיי זאָלט איהר ניט קלערען

איך האָף פאַר נעקסטען עלעקשאָן וועט עלעקטעט ווערען.

Herring mit Potaties

Words and music
Isidore Lillian

First verse from the songsheets:

In New York az ir vilt do a lebn makhn
Az eyner pedlt mit kalibatn zolt ir fun im nit lakhn
Oyb ir vilt geyn in biznes, zolt ir shnel nit loyfn
Efnt uf a stor un shtelt aroys a 'sayn' un fangt on tsu farkoyfn

Hot ver fun aykh a shlekhtn mogn un er ken nit kayen
Hot ver fun aykh keyn apetit nit un ken nit fardayen
Loyft nit tsu keyn doktor, dort ligt nit ayer yeshueh
Far a shlekhtn mogn hob ikh di beste refueh

A ganev shpet bay nakht is in a hoyz arayngekrokhn
Di tir bald geefnt un di 'safe' ufgebrokhn
Ven her hot di 'safe' geefnt iz er shir arop fun zinen,
Gemeynt hot er az dort ligt geld, tsum sof hot er gefinen:

Mayn shkheyne geyt tsu kind, di koyles geyn biz in 'siling'
A doktor zogt az zi hot shver iz pozitiv a tsviling
A tsveyter doktor hot ir bald far fir kinder geshvorn
Ven zi iz gelegn veyst ir vos zi hot geborn:

In yidishn teater hob ikh shoyn gezen a sakh 'piesn'
Di nemen zaynen di zelbe ikh vel zey nisht fargesn
Der shvartser yid, Dos pintele yid, ale dos veysn
Far vos zol a shrayber nit makhn a piese zi zol heysn...

Es kumt dokh an 'elekshon' dan zolt ir zikh nit mishn
Demokratn, Repoblikaner zoln zikh shlogn kop in kishn
Ruzvelt, Teft un Mister Vilson, fun zey zolt ir nit klern
Ikh hof far neкstn elekshon vet elektet vern

In New York, if you want to make a living
Don't laugh at somebody who's peddling sausage
If you want to go into business, you should quickly run
Open up a store and put up a sign, and begin to sell:

Herring with potatoes, herring with potatoes!
Don't bother with meat, steak, duck,
sponge cake and cheese cake
Chicken is a dog, compared to this, obviously!
The best dish for the belly is - herring with potatoes!

Eat what you want, it won't annoy me
The Hungarian eats goulash, the Galitsianer flesh in season
Romanians eat corn pudding, the goyim eat crabs
The Germans eat sauerkrat. What do the Litvaks eat?

Does anyone have a bad stomach and can't chew?
Does anybody suffer lack of appetite and can't digest?
Don't run to a doctor, your salvation doesn't lie there
For a bad stomach, I have the best cure

Late at night a thief crept into a house
He'd soon opened the door and cracked the safe
When he opened the safe he almost lost his mind
He thought there'd be gold lying there, but instead he found:

My neighbor went to childbed, her shouts rose to the ceiling
A doctor said it positively was going to be twins
A second doctor soon swore it would be quadruplets
When she delivered, guess what she bore?

In the Yiddish theater I've already seen a lot of shows
The names are sort of the same, I'm not going to forget them
"The Swarthy Jew," "The pintele Yid," everybody knows those
Why shouldn't a writer make a show that will be called:

An election is coming as you know, you shouldn't get into it
Democrats, Republicans, they're going to slog it out
Roosevelt, Taft and Mr. Wilson, you shouldn't know about them
I hope for the next election they elect:

BEWARE GIRLS!

הוט אייך
מיידלעך

INTRODUCED BY

DORA WEISSMAN

In the Sensational Drama

אן אויג פאר אן אויג

By ANSHEL SCHORR

At the Arch St. Theatre, Philadelphia, Pa.

Music by
SAMUEL SECUNDA

Sung by DORA WEISSMAN

Words by
ANSHEL SCHORR

Published By
J. & J. KAMMEN,
BROOKLYN, NEW YORK.

Hit eich Meidlich

Lyrics by
ANSHEL SCHORR

Music by
SAMUEL SECUNDA

Ikh benk nokh der East Side

Jacob Jacobs

Alexander Olshanetsky

Jews used to come from the whole world
To the East Side
As soon as they left Castle Garden
They'd set up in the East Side
There, newbies were taken care of very well
From the ship they were taken straight to the bath
After that, their necks were washed
Soon after, they were treated with bitter salts

I long for the East Side of yesteryear
Where everything bloomed endlessly
Everybody spoke Yiddish there
You were heartened by every word
It was just like in Israel
Maybe you are living a rich life now
But it still pulls at your heart
One pines for the East Side of the past

Ikh vel shoyn mer nit ganvenen

A fey-gl iz ge-floy-gn i-ber di de-kher i-ber di de-kher mit mayn me-lo-khe bin ikh me-ze-kher kh' vel shoyn mer nit gan-ve-nen nor ne-men nor-ne-men

vel shoyn mer nit gan-ve-nen nor ne-men ne-men

kh'hob far keynem keyn moyre keyn bushe (shame)
vayl mayn profesie kumt mir beyerushe (by inheritance)

Az ikh bin geven a nar un hot nisht folgn mayn tatn
Haynt zits ikh in turme un kuk aroys durkh di kratn

kh'bin arayngekrokhn in a fentster, kh'bin gevorn royt
m'hot mikh gekhapt un geshlogn shir tsum toyt

fli-zhe mayn feygele iber di kshakes (shrubs)
gib op mayne grusn di varshever bosiakes (vagrants)

kh'bin geven af di fray, loz ikh zikh hemder presn
un az ikh kum in kutshement arayn tut mir di vantsn esn

reboyne shel oylem ikh shver dir aleyn:
kh'vel aroyskumen fun pavyak, vel ikh ganvenen nisht geyn

kh'vel aroyskumen fun tfise, vel ikh geyn in dayn shteyger:
Dem ershtn potshontik a goldenem zeyger (order of business)

A feygl iz gefloygn iber di dekher iber di dekher
Mit mayn melokhe bin ikh mezekher

kh' vel shoyn mer nit ganvenen, nor nemen!

kh'hob far keynem keyn moyre keyn bushe (shame)
vayl mayn profesie kumt mir beyerushe (by inheritance)

Az ikh bin geven a nar un hot nisht folgn mayn tatn
Haynt zits ikh in turme un kuk aroys durkh di kratn

kh'bin arayngekrokhn in a fentster, kh'bin gevorn royt
m'hot mikh gekhapt un geshlogn shir tsum toyt

fli-zhe mayn feygele iber di kshakes (shrubs)
gib op mayne grusn di varshever bosiakes (vagrants)

kh'bin geven af di fray, loz ikh zikh hemder presn
un az ikh kum in kutshement arayn tut mir di vantsn esn

reboyne shel oylem ikh shver dir aleyn:
kh'vel aroyskumen fun pavyak, vel ikh ganvenen nisht geyn

kh'vel aroyskumen fun tfise, vel ikh geyn in dayn shteyger:
Dem ershtn potshontik a goldenem zeyger (order of business)

I'm not afraid or embarrassed in front of anyone
Because my profession came to me as an inheritance
I won't steal any more - I'll just take.

Because I was a fool and didn't obey my father
Now I'm sitting in jail looking through the bars

I crawled in through a window but I got caught red-handed
They grabbed me and beat me nearly to death

Fly over the shrubs, my little bird,
Give my greetings to the vagrants in Warsaw

When I was free, I got my shirts pressed
Now that I'm in the pokey, the bedbugs eat me

Master of the Universe, I myself swear to you:
If I get out of the slammer, I won't steal any more

If I get out of the joint, I'll walk in Your ways
(The first order of business: a gold watch!)

אין 100 יאהר ארום

IN 100 YOHR ARIM

Song from Thomashefsky's Musical Comedy "Upstairs and Down Stairs" Sung by Sam Kastin

Words by D. MEYEROWITZ

Music by J. M. RUMSHISKY

Catalogue of Celebrated Jewish Music for Piano with words

THE SWEETEST WALTZ EVER PUBLISHED

A POETS VISION. VALSE. in D minor (Medium Grade) by J. S. Deutsch. Published by A. Teres, 159 Delancey St. N.Y. price 20 cts. net.

Copyright MCMXII by A. Teres International Copyright secured,

Copyright MCMXII by A. Teres International Copyright secured

Published by A. TERES MUSIC DEALER and PUBLISHER 159 Delancey St., New York

Freyt aykh kinder es kumt a naye tsayt
Hert a vunder es vet bald zayn 'alrayt.'
Ir darf aykh gor nit zorgn, nit umgeyn tsudult
Es kumt bald on der morgn, ir krigt dan vos ir vilt.

Vos a mol kon reydn vos eyn oyg nor zet
Frank un fray far yedn ir darft nor ton a bet.
Ikh aleyn vel aykh dos gebn, ikh shver aykh do atsind
Oyb ikh vel es nor derlebn un kh'vel nor zayn gezunt.

In hundert yor arum, in hundert yor arum
Brenen vet men dan a velt on a groshn gelt, Oy!
Mit mayn mamen volt ikh yetst gehat dem grestn
shtrayt
Ver hot zi gebetn zi zol mir hobn far der tsayt?
In hundert yor arum s'volt nit gevezn krum
Ven zi volt mikh gehat in hundert yor arum

Fun London biz Niu York vet kostn bloyz a daym.
Aheym vet men forn bloyz far dinnertime
Shabes nokh dem kugl vet nit zayn vos tsu ton
vet men khapn a por fligl un a jump glaykh keyn
Berlin.

Tsu a matinee show vet men flien keyn Frentz
Un bay nakht in Turkey to a Salome dentz.
Gevald! aza min fargenign oy ikh es zikh uf,
vayl ikh vel shoyn damolt lign mit di tseyn aruf!

Shkheynim veln zikh nit krign mer
Un far eyn mark vet men krign a shok eyer
Vayber veln zayn gezunt un dik
Un kinder vet men hobn tsu 30-40 shtik
Meydlekh veln mer nit darfn keyn nadn
Vayl af yedn ort vet zikh valgern a man
Keyn sandek un keyn moyel vet nit zayn in yener tsayt
Vayl yinglekh veln geboyrn vern fartikerhayt

Shvues tsum seder vet men zingen zmires
Un in Vilne vet men krign gor umziste dires
Daytshland un Frankraykh veln lebn besholem
Der mark un der dolar veln hobn eyn ponim
Kaptsonim un gvirim es vet nit zayn keyn kine
Ale meysim vet men bafrayen fun danine.
Akhtsik yorike vayber vet men nemen far soldatn
Un in Seym veln betlekh shteyn far di shlofedike
deputatn!

Rejoice, kids, a new era is coming. Listen, it's a wonder: things are gonna be ok. You don't need to worry, don't go around in a tizzy. Tomorrow's coming soon! You'll get what you want. What you talk about, what an eye can see, It'll be free for everybody if you just ask. I myself will give it to you, I swear to you here and now If I can just survive till then with my health intact!

A hundred years from now, a hundred years from now We'll be able to have a high old time without even a penny, oy! I'd have quite the bone to pick with my mother now: Who told her she should have me so many years too early? A hundred years from now ... it wouldn't have been bad at all If she'd had me a hundred years from now.

Getting from London to New York will cost only a dime. You'll just travel home for dinner. Shabbes after the kugl, if you're bored You'll grab a couple of wings and jump straight to Berlin You'll be able to fly to France for a matinee And then be in Turkey that night for a Salome dance. Gee! I'd eat up a pleasure like that, Except I'll already lying teeth up in the ground.

Neighbors won't fight any more You'll be able to buy 60 eggs for one mark Wives will be stout and healthy, folks will have 13 or 14 children. Girls won't need dowries any more because there'll be men hanging around everywhere. The circumcision experts won't be needed then Because baby boys will be born pre-snipped.

People will be singing table songs from Shavuot to Passover In Vilna folks will be getting apartments for free Germany and France will live in peace, The mark and the dollar will look the same. Poor people and rich people? There'll be no jealousy. All corpses will be freed from paying taxes. Eighty year old women will be taken for soldiers And in Parliament there'll be beds for the sleepy deputies

In hundert yor arum

I. Kh. Glezer

Freyt aykh kin-der es kumt a na-ye tsayt Hert a vun-der es vet bald zayn 'al-
Fun London biz Niu York vet kost-n bloyz a daym. A-heym vet men for-n bloyz far din-ner

rayt.' ir darf aykh gor nit zor-gn nit um-geyn tsu-dult es kumt bald on der
time Sha-bes nokh dem ku-gl vet nit zayn vos tsu ton vet men khap-n a por

mor-gn ir krigt dan vos ir vilt. Vos a mol kon rey-dn vos eyn oyg nor zet
fligl un a jump glaykh keyn Ber-lin. Tsu a ma-ti-nee show vet men flien keyn Frentz

Frank un fray far ye-dn ir darft nor ton a bet. Ikh a-leyn vel aykh dos gebn, ikh
Un bay nakht in Tur-key to a Salo-me dentz Ge-vald! a-za min far-ge-ni-gn

shver aykh do a-tsind Oyb ikh vel es nor der-lebn un kh'vel nor zayn ge-zunt.
oy ikh es zikh uf, vayl ikh vel shoyn da-molt li-gn mit di tseyn a-ruf!

In hun-dert yor a-rum In hun-dert yor a-rum Bre-nen vet men dan a velt on a gro-shn gelt, Oy!

Mit mayn ma-men volt ikh yetst ge hat dem grest-n shtrayt verhot zi ge-be-tn zi zol mir hob-n far der tsayt.

In hun-dert yor a-rum s'volt nit ge-ve-zn krum ven zi volt mikh ge-hat in hun-dert yor a-rum

In hundert yor arum p2

I. Kh. Glezer

63

"לעבען זאל קאלומבוס!"

"LEBEN SOL COLUMBUS"

WORDS BY BORIS THOMASHEWSKY.

MUSIC BY PERLMUTTER AND WOHL.

"LEBEN SOL COLUMBUS!"
FROM SHOMER'S COMEDY
"THE GREEN MILLIONAIRE"
Produced by BORIS THOMASHEWSKY
At The NATIONAL THEATRE, NEW YORK

"לעבען זאל קאלומבום!"
פון שמר'ס פעריהמטע קאמעדי
"דער גרינער מיליאנער"
געשפיעלט מיט גרויס סוקסעס
אין טאמאשעווסקי'ס נעשאנאל טהעאטער

⤙ PUBLISHED BY A.TERES ⤚
· MUSIC DEALER AND PUBLISHER ···
88 DELANCEY ST. NEW YORK ·

Long Live Columbus!

America, what a town, what a wonder, I swear! God's presence rests on you, we should live this way. Wars, guns, human blood, we don't need that misery. A governor or a tsar? Completely unnecessary. Oh, it's good! Everybody sing together:

Long life to Columbus! Drink a toast, brothers. Long life to Columbus and to this new land. Be happy, don't believe the blowhards. Shout it out, Jews: Long live Columbus!

A slander's been cooked up against one of our Jews; a devil made music and Hamen played the fiddle. The lawyers, however, won't be silenced, they'll bring out the truth. Believe me, Noah, it will turn out well: they won't hang a Jew! Oy, it's good! Jews, sing with me:

In Washington it isn't quiet, Burnett is singing a song He wants to make a new bill, a misfortune for the Jews. But Wilson doesn't want it! Just shut up, Burnett! Jews, come, it will be well, you'll be good brothers!

Another verse:

Far meydlekh iz Ameritshke a glik, nor a ganeydn,
Vayl boyes iz do kekhol hayam a tayneg, oy, a lebn,
Un keyn nadn darf men nit, shadkhonim af kapores,
Un az a trombenik vil gelt, krigt er a moyd mit tsores!
Ay s'iz gut, zingt zhe, meydlekh, mit:

America is happiness, paradise for girls:
Boys here are plentiful like the sands of the sea,
a pleasure! What a life!

Long live Franz Josef & Wilhelm!

We Jews can go dancing, we've gotten revenge. The German is burying Nicholas now, deep in the earth. Franz Josef is beating him too, everybody knows. Little Nicholas has cramps in his belly, he's in hot water. Oh, this is fine! Shout, Jews, big and small:

Long life to Franz Josef and the German, Wilhelm. They're making soup out of the Russian fool. Rejoice, Jews, wish them success! Let Nikolai and his family be the sacrifice.

Nicholas wanted to swallow up Galitsiye. Now he's being driven to the devil - he's running, he's exploding. He's running from Warsaw, he's leaving Brisk. As soon as he stands still he takes one in the muzzle, the German drags him to school. Oh, this is fine! Shout, Jews, big and small:

The Russian and his soldiers have been proud for years, but long life to the German leader, he's hitting them from all sides. Franz Josef is also giving good blows, he too can deliver. He shoots with a full pot of potatoes, he captures cossacks. Oh, this is fine! Shout, Jews, big and small:

Little Nicholas strove to eat Vienna sausage. He's lived to see a plague, he's stabbed in the side. The idiot ran away to the church to beg for blessings. His God really helped him out: he got blows and an ague. Oh, this is fine! Shout, Jews, big and small:

LEBEN SOL COLUMBUS

Sung by Mr. Thomashefsky and Mr. Blank

Words by
B. THOMASHEFSKY

Music by
PERLMUTTER - WOHL

Andantino

A -me-ritch-ke a mdi na le a me-cha-ia ch'le-ben es riht auf ihr a shchi-ne -'le mir zol-len a -soi le-ben Mil - chò-mes bik-sen men-schen blut dar-fen mir auf tzo-res a gu-ber-na-tor dorf men nit a kai-ser auf ka - po-res oi s'is gut singt sze yid-den mit Oi

II

A bilbul hot men ausgetracht   Die lawyers aber schweigen nit
Auf unser'n a Yiddel,   Dem emes aroiszubreingen,
A nigger hut music gemacht   Gloib mir Neiach, es wet sein gut,
Un Hamman shpielt dem fiddel!   A Yiddel wet nit heingen!
                                    Oi, s'is gut, singt sze Yidden mit mir mit!

III

In Washington is gor nit shtill   Aber Wilson will das nit,
Burnett singt a liedel,   Mach, Burnett, kein gerider,
Ehr will machen a naiem bill   Yiddlach kumt, es wet sein gut
Ein umglick far'n Yiddel!   Ihr seint gutte bridder!

CHORUS.

Lebn zol Franz Yozef un Wilhelm

Mir yid-n meg-n tan-tsn geyn mir hob-n a ne-ko-me Der
Daytsh ba-grobt yetst Ni-ko-lai tif in der a-do-me Franz Jo-sef shlogt im oykh dos
veyst fun aykh a ye-der Ni-ko-lay-ke hot kremps in boykh, er
krigt yetst hey-se be-der Oy vi dos iz fayn shrayt ye-der groys un kleyn
Leb-n zol Franz Jo-sef un mit dem Daytsh Wil-helm zey
ko-khn yetst a ros-l fun dem ka-tsap dem khe-lem Freyt aykh, yi-dn,
vinsht zey ma-zl bro-khe a ka-po-re Ni-ko-lay-ke mit zayn mish-po-khe

Gevolt hot Nikolayke gor Galitsiye aynshlingen
Yetst traybt men im tsum shvartsn yor er loyft, er vert tsespringen
Aroys fun Varshe aroys fun Brisk azoy loyft er keseyder
Koym blaybt er shteyn krigt er in pisk der Daytsh shlept im in kheyder
Oy vi dos iz fayn, shrayt yidn groys un kleyn!

Shtoltsirt hot yorn der katsap mit zayne soldatn
Nor lebn zol a daytsher kop, er shlogt zey fun ale zaytn
Franz Yoysef git oykh [gute] klep er ken oykh gut derlangen
Er shist mit bulbes gantse tep kazakn nemt er gefangen
Oy vi dos iz fayn, shrayt yidn groys un kleyn

Nikolayke hot nor geshtrebt tsu esn a viner bratn
A make hot er dos derlebt, a shtekhenis in di zaytn
Gelofn iz der idiot in kloyster betn brokhes
Geholfn take hot im zayn Got, er krigt klep mit kadokhes
Oy vi dos iz fayn, shrayt yidn groys un kleyn

Malle vus men Redt auf dem Stoop

מאלע וואָס מען רעדט אויף דעם סטוּף

From M. Richter's Play— The TWO MOTHERS-IN-LAW Die TZWEI SHWEEGERS

Words and Music by LOUIS FRIEDSELL
Sung by Mrs. B. TOMASCHEFSKY

CELEBRATED JEWISH MUSIC FOR PIANO WITH WORDS

Published by A. TERES
Music Dealer and Publisher
159 DELANCEY STREET, NEW YORK

MALLE VUS MEN REDT AUF DEM STOOP

Sung by Mrs. B. Tomaschefsky

Words and Music
by LOUIS FRIEDSELL

3

Chorus Allegretto moderato

Malle vus men redt auf dem stoop
Recorded by Anna Hoffman in 1918

Vilt ir hern zakhn tsum veynen un tsum lakhn
Vos nor in undzer veltl tut zikh op?
Yo men redt, yo men redt af dem stoop.

Redt eyner nor shtusim
Dertseylt men shoyn bald nisim
Fun gornit vert bashafn a loop-di-loop
Yo men redt, yo men redt af dem stoop

Plutsim zogt aykh a yid, un shvert heylik git
Fun der rebetsin a sod er aykh dertseylt
Az gezen hot er grod, durkh a shpeltl in bod (slot)
Az eyn milkhedike zayt ir felt

Male vos men redt af dem stoop
Male vos es tut zikh dort op
Men hert dort a vits, a shpas un a lakh,
Men redt dortn on a sakh un a sakh.
Male vos men redt af dem stoop
Male vos es tut zikh dort op. Hey!
Men redt af ir on a shir
Men redt af mir, me ret af dir
Men redt af aykh, men redt af dem stoop

In Coney Island kimen - tsu bodn zikh un
shvimen
Fil boyes, meydlekh, es tut zikh dortn op
Yo men redt, yo men redt af dem stoop
Men halt zikh dort in vitslen
Un eyns dem tsveytn kitslen
Es tut zikh ven men bodt zikh bay dem sloop
Yo men redt yo men redt af dem stoop

Oftmol treft zikh a shpas, a madam vi a fas,
Vert freylekh un bakumt fil mut.
Varft mit hent un mit fis,
Shpringt un tantst zo lang biz
Trakh! Es platst der gantser beyding suit.

Want to hear things happening in our little world that'll make you cry and laugh? People are talking on the stoop. One's talking nonsense, they're talking about miracles. From nothing, they create a loop-de-loop! Yes, they're talking on the stoop.

Suddenly somebody tells you, he makes a holy vow, he tells a secret about the rebetsin... That through a crack in the bathhouse wall he saw she was missing a [?]

There's no telling what they'll say on the stoop. Who knows what happens there? You'll hear a wisecrack, a joke and a laugh. People talk an awful lot there.

There's no telling what they'll say on the stoop. Who knows what happens there? They talk about her on and on, they talk about me, they talk about you, they talk about everyone on the stoop.

Lots of boys and girls come to Coney Island to bath and swim and fool around. Yes, they talk on the stoop. People are always joking, tickling each other, it happens when they're bathing by the sloop. Yes, they talk on the stoop.

There's often something to laugh about. A lady built like a barrel gets happy and exuberant. She throws her hands and feet around, she jumps around and dances until Sploof! Her whole bathing suit explodes.

MEN HOIDET ZICH IN AMERICA
(SWING DAYS)

מען הוידעלט זיך אין אמעריקא

FROM THE OPERETTA:
"A MENSH ZOL MEN ZEIN"
or "ABRAHAM HASHKENAZI"
THE SUCCESS OF THREE LEADING
NEW YORK THEATRES:
"WINDSOR", "PEOPLES" and
"NEW STAR"

פאן דער אפערעטא:
"א מענש זאל מען זיין"
אדער "אברהם השכנזי"
געשפיעלט מיט גרוים ערפאלג
אין די 3 גרעסטע ניריארקער
אידישע טהעאטערע
"ווינדזאר", "פיפלם" "ניו סטאר"

PUBLISHED FOR
PIANO SOLO
WITH WORDS
VIOLIN or
MANDOLIN.

WORDS BY
A. SCHOR

MUSIC BY
PERLMUTTER
AND
WOHL

MR. PERLMUTTER

SONG HITS OF THE PLAY:
1) A MENSH ZOL MEN ZEIN — א מענש זאל מען זיין
2) THERE'S A SECRET — ס'איז דא א סוד דערבייא
3) SWING DAYS — מען הוידעלט זיך אין אמעריקא

Published by A. TERES, Music Dealer & Publisher
240½ E. HOUSTON ST., NEW YORK

MR. WOHL

73

Men hoydet zikh

Anshel Shor & Joseph Tanzman

Perlmutter & Wohl 1908

Shmiel Yan - kl kumt tsu geyn   Es rasht zikh gor in der shtot   In A - me - ri-
Dos er - shte af der shif   hoyd-n zikh fun kleyn biz groys.   In a New

ca   ge - ven   Er trogt zikh a "la - test style suit."   "Vos hert zikh e - pes
Yor - ker car   Oy hoy-det di kish-kes a - roys.   Men fort in Co - ney

dort?"   fregt men im   gor on of - her   "Fregt nit? ent - fert er, "Men
Isle   zikh hoy - dn   mit a gir   a sheyns   men hot cha - se - ne men

hoy-det zikh dort un nit mer."   Hoy - da, hoy - da,   men hoy-det zikh
ho - det in   vi - gl a kleyns.

her un a - hin   Hoy - da hoy - da   meg men zayn gel tsi grin

muz men zikh hoy - dn,   hoy - dn,   dort in a shop baym ma - shin.   Men

hoy-det dos le - bn a - roys   biz es gey-en di koy - khes oys.

74

Shmiel Yankl kumt tsu geyn es rasht zikh gor in der shtot
In America geven Er trogt zikh a "latest style suit."
"Vos hert zikh epes dort?" fregt men im gor on ofher
"Fregt nit? entfert er, "Men hoydet zikh dort un nit mer."

Hoyda, hoyda, men hoydet zikh her un ahin
Hoyda hoyda meg men zayn gel tsi grin
Muz men zikh hoydn, hoydn, dort in a shop baym mashin.
Men hoydet dos lebn aroys biz es geyen di koykhes oys.

Dos ershte af der shif hoydn zikh fun kleyn biz groys.
In a New Yorker car oy hoydet di kishkes aroys.
Men fort in Coney Isle zikh hoydn mit a girl a sheyns
Men hot chasene men hodet in vigl a kleyns.

Shmiel Yankl comes along, there is a hubbub in town:
He was in America, he wears the latest style suit.
"What's the news from over there?" people are always asking him
"Don't ask," he says, "All they do is swing there."

Swing, they swing this way and that
Swing, you could get seasick
You have to swing, there in a shop by the machine,
You swing your life out until you lose your strength

So to start off, on the ship everybody large and small sways
In a New York trolley car, oy, you sway till your guts fall out
You go to Coney Island to swing there with a pretty girl
You get married, you rock a little one in the cradle

S'iz do gold un briliantn in der gantser velt
Tsirung diamantn un oykh a sakh gelt
Sheyne raykhe kleyder un heyzer gor a prakht
Trakht ir nor keseyder far raykhe iz dos gemakht
Es volt nit badarft zayn orem oder raykh
Men volt es badarft aynteyln yeder glaykh
volt der oriman nit geshrign a sakh

Men ken lebn nor men lozt nit (2x)
Eyner tsufil hot un es geyt im gut un fayn
Men ken lebn nor men lozt nit (2x)
Di velt belongt tsu Got un yedn darf gut zayn

Mayn shokhns vayb iz a sheyne
un mayn vayb iz zeyer mies
Un a shnur hot er a sheyne iz zi vi tsuker zis
Vi ikh gey nor ze ikh vayber sheyn on shir
Un mit a mies vayb ikh bagey zikh
un mies zikh haltn mit ir
Freg ikh, vi lang ken dos azoy geyn
Ven ikh ze ba yenem a vayb vos iz sheyn
Veyn ikh zikh git oys un zog tsu zikh aleyn, oy,

Men ken lebn nor men lozt nit (2x)
Eyn emes iz tsu sheyn un dem tsveytens tzu mies gor
Men ken lebn nor men lozt nit (2x)
Men darf makhn a gezets zey tsu "chendzhn" yedes yor

Ot hot ir prohibition do bay undz in land
Mentshn zoln zikh mishn, is dos nit a shand
Trinken geyt men shtern, vos iz dos far a kunts?
Un punkt di vos farvern trinken
Trinken nokh merer fun undz
Men darf loyfn flien makhn a geshrey
Un ot di verter darf men zogn zey:
Ver ken trinken azoy fil kave ken trinken azoy fil tey...

Men ken lebn nor men lozt nit (2x)
Vos iz dos far a "show," vos iz dos far a "trick"
Men ken lebn nor men lozt nit (2x)
Men darf endern di "law" un undz gebn bronfn tsurik

There's gold and diamonds in the world, diamond jewelry and a lot of money, beautiful fine clothes and lovely houses. You are just thinking all the time: this comes of money. There shouldn't be poor or rich. Everyone should be equal, then the poor man would not be wailing:

You could live, but they don't let you. One has too much and everything goes well for him. You could live, but they don't let you. The world belongs to God and everyone should be good.

My neighbor's wife is beautiful while my wife is very ugly. And he has a pretty daughter-in-law who is sugar sweet. Wherever I go I see loads of pretty women. I'm committed to an ugly wife and must stay with her. I ask, how long can this go on? When I see everybody else has a pretty wife I cry out heartily and say to myself:

You could live, but they don't let you. One's wife is too pretty, another's is too ugly. You could live, but they don't let you. A law should be made to exchange them every year.

Now we have Prohibition in the land. Isn't it a shame people are interfering? They're preventing drinking, what kind of trick is that? And exactly the ones who forbid drinking drink even more than we do. We should go run, make an outcry, and we should say these exact words to them: Who can drink so much coffee, who can drink so much tea?

You could live, but they don't let you. What kind of show is this, what kind of trick? You could live, but they don't let you. They should end the law and give us back our booze.

Men Kon Leben,
Nor Men Lost Nit.

Words and Music by
GUS. GOLDSTEIN
arr. by *Jack Kammen*

Men Kon Leben 2

Words By.
Morris Rund.

© CIE704592

(MEN KEN LEBEN NOR MEN LOST NIT)

Music By.
Joseph Rumshinsky

ich be tracht di velt vi mis si is ge shtelt ich zug aich plein as

mir ge felt si gur nit vil ei ner tun a sach kimt zu a zbei ter

glaich in shtrait ge vald di veist doch as me tur nit ven mit a frau ich

red ich kish si in ich glet misht men zich a rain in mi ten

Chorus

me lost mich nit za chet me ken le ben nor me lost nit se macht

jei den beis in des kos tet du nit geh du nit shtei du nit red

du nit glet jei der gur nit sugt me tur nit ch'veis nit far vus

nein vie ken lei ben nor me lost nit bald ert ir shra en

ai ge vald es past nit ch'sei a moid shen in roit ful mit

chein nu alt dich ain me ken le ben shein nor me lost nit

nein

Peysakh Burstein recorded this different song by the same name, written by Morris Rund and Joseph Rumshinsky.

Ikh batrakht di velt vi mies zi iz geshtelt
Ikh zog aykh 'plain' az mikh/r gefelt zi gurnit
Vil eyner tuen a sakh, kumt tsu a tsveyter glaykh
Un shrayt "gevald, du veyst dokh az me tor nit!"
Ven mit a froy ikh red, ikh kush zi un ikh glet,
Misht men zikh arayn in mitn, me lost aykh/mikh nit s'z'a khet!

Me ken lebn nor me lozt nit
Es makht yedn beyz un 'deskostet' (shrayt yeder gevald es past nit)
Do nisht gey, dort nisht shtey, do nit red, dort nit glet
Yeder gornit zogt me tor nit, kh'veys nit far vos. Neyn
Me ken lebn nor me lozt nit
Bald est ir shrayen "oy gevald es past nit"
Kh'say/derze/me zet a mod, sheyn un royt,
Ful mit kheyn, nu alt dikh eyn halt dikh ayn
me ken lebn sheyn nor me lozt nit.

I think about the world, how ugly it is,
I tell you plainly, I don't like it at all
If you want to do something, somebody comes right along
And shouts "Gevald, you know it's forbidden!"
When I talk with a woman, I kiss her and caress her,
People interfere right in the middle of things, "You can't, it's a sin!"

You could live but they don't let you
It makes everybody angry and disgusted (everyone shouts, it's not suitable)
Don't go here, don't stand there, don't talk, don't caress
Any nobody tells you it's forbidden, I don't know why
You could live but they don't let you

מוזיק אלבום
MUSIC ALBUM

מען וועט דיר
ניט מיטגעבען אין קבר.
פֿון א. שאָר.

MEN WET DIR
NIT MITGEBEN IN KEIVER.

By A. SHOR.

Music by JOS. BRODY

HEBREW PUBLISHING CO.
50 ELDRIDGE ST.   NEW YORK

J. KELLER

Men vet dir nit mitgebn pı

Anshel Shor

Joseph Brody

Men vet dir nit mitgebn

S'iz geven a mol a groyser gvir,
Keyn oreman nit gelozt af zayn tir
Zayn gantses lebn af der velt
Iz geven nor gelt, nor gelt
Geroybt, gerisn, gor on gevisn
hot der shlekhter yid,
Un ven es iz gekumen zayn letste sho
Un men firt im shoyn in zayn eybiker ru
Hert men vi a "bas kol" zingt im dos troyer lid

Tell me, answer me this: Why is everything too little for you? Nothing's too hard when it comes to getting richer. However much you have, you want even more.

You suffocate the poor man, you oppress the worker. You never get tired of flaying.

But when your last minute arrives Good brother, things won't be very good for you, Then they'll sing you a sad song:

Honor and money were your world, you sought so much honor. You strove most of all to become rich. But when your time is here, even if you're rich, You're not given anything to bring into the grave with you.

There once was a big rich man, he didn't let any poor man in his door. His whole life in the world was just money. He robbed and razed without conscience, that evil guy. And when his last hour came and he was carried to his eternal rest A heavenly voice sang him this sad song:

A mentsh ken dokh makhn a mol a toes

This song was found at the Copyright Office.

I have a lot of jobs, I'm running around everywhere
I get so addled I don't know what to do
Well, and so what? A person obviously makes a mistake once in a while.

So, I was the "Reverend" presiding at a wedding
I forgot what I was doing and made the blessing for circumcision
Well, so? So sometimes a person makes makes a mistake!

So the bridegroom gets mad and shouts that I'm a drunkard
The bride's mother says: "They're cutting me into pieces!"
Well, come on, big deal. Sometimes you make a mistake.

Then, in addition: yesterday, like a big clay dummy,
Instead of going to a circumcision, I went all the way to the cemetery!

My wife goes into labor, my mother-in-law suddenly gets sick at the same time
So I was the nurse and went to get her some medicine.

Oy! The mother-in-law starts shrieking, she's burning like a thousand flames
So the doctor says: I could absolutely have poisoned her!

The doctor gets really mad, he's dead pale with fury!
"What's this? I told you to give her the pill in water."

He said "give her the pill in water," but I didn't understand,
So I put the pill in her mouth and sat her down in the bathtub.

87

A mentsh ken dokh makhn a toes

Ikh hob a sakh me - lo - khes ikh loyf a - her a - hin ikh ver a - zoy tse - dult az ikh veys nit vos tsu ton nu es vues nu iz vues a mentsh ken dokh makhn a mol a to - es Nu! Bin ikh af a kha - se - ne der Rev - e - rend ge - zis far - ges ikh zikh nokh un makh gor dort di bro - khe fun a bris nu es vues nu iz vues a mentsh ken dokh makhn a mol a to - es vert in kas der kho - sn un shrayt ikh bin a shi - ker zogt der ka - les ma - me: "Zey tse - shnay - dn mikh af shti - ker!" nu es

A mentsh ken dokh makhn a mol a toes

ORIGINAL TERES EDITION

א מענש זאל מען זיין

◄ A MENSH ZOL MEN ZEIN ►

Mme BERTHA KALISH   MME R. PRAGER

LOUIS FRIEDSELL   S. MOGULESKO   A. GOLDFADEN   J. ADLER   J. BRODY

LIST OF
CELEBRATED JEWISH COMPOSITIONS
FOR PIANO AND VOICE

B. THOMASHEFSKY   B. BERNSTEIN

J. M. RUMSHINSKY   DAVID KESSLER

S. SCHMULEWITZ   K. JUVELIER

*1 A MENSH ZOL MEN ZEIN.
*2 A BREEVELE DER MAMMEN.
*3 DUS TALESIL.
*4 ICH BENK A HAIM (Dus Faigele).
*5 AL TASHLICHENU.
*6 GOTT UND ZEIN MISHPET IS GERECHT.
*7 SHOLEM BEIAS.
*8 DUS LEBEDIGE YESOIMELE.
9 ELEND IZ DER MENSH—
    —WOS FARLOZT ZEIN HAIM
*10 DUS SHAIFELE.
*11 VE-YITEN LECHO.
12 DEE BLOOMEN KRENTZELE.
*13 ISRULIK KOOM A HAIM.
*14 LEBEDIG UND FREILACH.
*15 DUS YUSEMIL (from Ben Ami).
16 DEE NESHOME FOON MEIN FOLK.
17 DUS FERTRIBENE TEIBELE
*18 YIDELACH BRIDERLACH.
19 VEN MEN ROOFT DIR TZURIK.
20 VER ES GRUBT OIF YENEM A GRUB
21 OUF'N PREEPETSHOK.
22 UNZER REBENU
23 ICH BIN A BOARDER BY MEIN WEIB
24 LAY SIWAYSHI WELAY SIKOLMI.
25 DEE YIDDISHE KROIN
26 SHULDIG BIST DU YIDELE ALAIN.
27 DEE MOOME GLEEKELE.
28 DEE TFEELEN.
29 MEN SHART GOLD IN AMERICA.
30 TATENU KOOM TZURIK A HAIM.
35 A MAME'S WERTH.
36 DEE FARLORENE SHAIFELE.
*37 DEM PASTACHL'S CHOLEM.
38 LEIDEN UND FREIDEN.
39 DEE LUSTIGE TZWEI.
41 TZUBROCHENE BEIMELACH.
42 A FOLK OHN A HAIM.
43 ELI ELI, ORIGINAL.
44 ELI ELI, ORIGINAL (Simplified).

*45 A MUTTER'S HARTZ.
46 SHLUF MEIN KEEND.
47 DUS BISELE GLICK.
48 NOCH A BISEL UND EPES NOCH.
*49 WEH DEM KEEND VEN A MAME—
50 EINEG SHABES.   —FEHLT.
51 FAMILIE GLICK.
52 TZURIK KEIN ZION (Back to Zion).
53 LEBEN ZOL COLUMBUS.
54 GEDENK MEIN KEEND
    DER MAMME'S TREHREN.
55 HEVEL HAVOLIM.
*56 KOL NIDRA, ORIGINAL.
57 KOL NIDRA, ORIGINAL (Simplified)
58 HATIKVOH (Jewish National Hymn).
59 MEIN KALE.
*60 DOO BIST A TATE TZU ALE GLEICH.
61 TATE MAME TEIERE.
62 SHENK MIR MEIN MAME.
64 GOTTENU GIEB ADREI DUS REDELE.
65 HEIBT FISLACH UND TREENKT—
    —LE-CHAYIM.
67 TZORES AUF DER ELTER.
68 MEIN LEEBSTER FREIND
    IZ MEIN MAMENU (A Mame's Leid)
72 WOO ZENNEN MEINE KEENDER.
73 ALES BEI DEM FETTER.
74 MALE WOS MEN REDT AUF'N STOOP
75 A KEEND IZ DUS GLICK AUF DER—
76 RUSSLAND.   —WELT.
78 OVEENU MALKEINU (David Kessler).
80 A CHAVER IN LEBEN.
*81 A KEEND OHN A HAIM.
82 ES FEHLT DEE MAME.
83 A KEEND'S GEBBET.
*84 IN 100 YOHR ARUM.
85 LEEBE TZU KEENDER (Keender Leebe).
87 IN HONIG LAND.
90 ES IZ A SUD DERBEI.
91 ITZEEK

* Indicates that the song is also published for Violin and Mandolin.

PRICE 30 CENTS NET, no discount

A. PERLMUTTER   HERMAN WOHL

Published by
DANIEL H. GREENBERG
Music Publisher
Successor and Publisher of the Famous "TERES EDITION"
157 DELANCEY ST., NEW YORK, N. Y.
MADE IN U.S.A.

Designed and Copyrighted by D. H. Greenberg 1920

A mentsh zol men zayn was the underlying tune for many parodies.
It is also known as "Mit gelt tor men nit shtoltsirn"

You think, when you're rich, that you're Master of the Universe
You think nobody's your equal, that nothing but money matters.
You think as soon as you're rich, folks owe you lots of respect.
The arrogant fool doesn't understand: money is round, it rolls away.
Today I have it, tomorrow you have it,
Later, other people have it.

You mustn't be proud that you have money,
It's easy to lose it.
Then you'll suddenly feel the bitterness of being a pauper.
If you want to earn a good name that will endure after your death
Don't brag about your fancy forefathers,
Just be a good person.

Little man, when things are going well and you're incredibly rich
Remember, don't forget the duty you have:
When a poor man comes to your house, don't let him leave with empty pockets
Because you can never predict what's going to happen
Someday it may happen to you, too
Today you're blessed, you're worth a lot, tomorrow it may be the opposite.

I once saw a man as rich as Korekh
He was proud and awful, he persecuted people all the time
Then times changed, the wheel turned
Then you could see that proud rich man begging: "Give me alms!"
Suffering more and more, his death so hard,
He lies buried in strangers' shrouds

A mentsh zol men zayn

Anshel Shor

Perlmutter & Wohl 1908

Ba - trakht dem mentsh ven er iz raykh vi er nor brent a velt_ Er meynt az key - ner
iz im glaykh, az al - es iz nor gelt Er meynt az koym iz er nor a ge - vir
kumt im shoyn ze - yer fil ko - ved da - fir un der shtolt - ser nar nit far - shteyt az gelt iz dokh rund un es
geyt Haynt iz es bay mir un morg-n bay dir un shpe - ter bay an - de - re fir. Mit
gelt tor men nit shtol - tsi - rn men ken es laykht far - li - rn dan ersht ken men
fi - ln dem bi - te - rn tam fun dem o - re - man vil - stu zikh a no - men der -
var - bn s'zol blay - bn nokh dayn shtar - bn varf a - vek dem
pus tn yi - khes a mentsh zols - tu nor zayn zayn.

Mentshele, ven dir geyt gut un du bist raykh on a shir
Gedenkzhe un farges nor nit di flikht vos ligt nokh af dir:
Az ven an oreman kumt in dayn hoyz
Leydik loz im fun dayn shtub nit aroys
Vayl du kenst faroys dos nit zen
Vos amol ken mit di oykh geshen
Haynt iz dir bashert, host du nokh a vert
Un morgn ken zayn gor farkert

Ikh hob shoyn a mol gezen a man vi Koyrekh raykh
Shtolts un shlekht iz er geven, geroydeft mentshn a sakh
Dan iz gekumen an ander tsayt, dos redele hot zikh ibergedreyt
Haynt, zet men dem shtoltsn gevir vi er bet: "A nedove shenkt mir"!
Gelitn nokh mer geshtarbn azoy shver
In fremde takhrikhim (shrouds) ligt er.

Mentshn-freser

Solomon Small 1916

In di lung-en tif ba-grob-n voynt di bla-se pest di ba-tsil-n di mi-krob-n boy-en zey-er nest fres-n und-zer layb un leb-n frukh-per-n zikh pek un mir muz-n zelbst far-shveb-n far der tsayt a-vek un mir fil-n vi mir gey-en shtil un lang-zam oys un di shmerts-n un di vey-en zay-nen shrek-lekh groys un di fin-ste-re makh-sho-ves gre-se-rn dem shmerts yor-n ligt der ma-lekh ha-mo-ves tif bay undz in herts. Mi-kro-bn ba-tsi-ln vos vilt ir? Zogt ve-mes shli-khes der-filt ir? Ir frest di kor-bo-nes gor on a rakh-mo-nes, in bli-yen-de leb-n nor tsilt ir! Ir bodt zikh in tre-rn fun vey-ner ir tsit oys di markh fun di bey-ner ir samt di ge-de-rem ir kri-khen-de ver-em, mi-krob-n ba-tsi-ln vos vilt ir?

94

In di lungen tif bagrobn voynt di blase pest
Di batsiln, di mikrobn boyen zeyer nest
Fresn undzer layb un lebn frukhpern zikh pek
Un mir muzn zelbst farshvebn far der tsayt avek
Un mir filn vi mir geyen shtil un langzam oys
Un di shmertsn un di veyen zaynen shreklekh groys
Un di finstere makhshoves gresern dem shmerts
Yorn ligt der malekh hamoves tif bay undz in herts.

Mikrobn batsiln vos vilt ir?
Zogt vemes shlikhes derfilt ir?
Ir frest di korbones gor on a rakhmones,
in bliyende lebn nor tsilt ir!
Ir bodt zikh in trern fun veyner
ir tsit oys di markh fun di beyner
Ir samt di gederem ir krikhende verim,
tmikrobn batsiln vos vilt ir?

Nokh a shreklikhe mageyfe geyt fun land tsu land
Mit di shnelkeyt fun a sreyfe fun a fayer-brand!
Kleyne kinder nemt es samen, eyfelekh fun brust
Roybt avek fun tatn-mamen zeyer lebens-lust
Makhtloz iz dem mentshns zinen, s'blaybt di khokhme shtil
S'iz keyn mitl tsu gefinen gegn a batsil!
Vos paralizirt di kinder, undzer lebns-shayn
Mir dervartn gotes vunder, s'zol dos mer nit zayn!

Kep gekroynte, diplomatn, um tsu hobn zig,
Tsvingen undz tsu zayn soldatn, traybn undz in krig!
Yunge mentshn in milionen tsoln zeyer prayz
Un es vert far di kanonen zeyer fleysh a shpayz!
Un tsukripelte, un toyte, faln do un dort
naye lebns ongegreyte filn oys dem ort
Un in groyse tife kvorim pakt men laykhes fil
Un di hersher, di keysorim, shpiln shakhmat shpil

The pale pestilence lives deeply buried in the lungs The bacilli, the microbes build their nest They gobble us up, body and soul, and multiply a lot And we must ourselves dwindle/fade away before our time And we feel how we're expiring quietly and slowly, and the suffering and crying are terribly great. And the dark thoughts increase the pain. For years the Angel of Death lies deep in our hearts.

Macrobes, bacilli, what do you want? Whose mission are you carrying out? You gobble the victims mercilessly, you aim only at blooming lives You bathe yourselves in the tears of those who weep, you suck the marrow from the bones You poison the entrails, you crawling worms. Microbes, bacilli, what do you want?

Another terrible epidemic goes from land to land With the speed of a blazing fire from a piece of burning wood. It poisons little children, infants at the breast, It robs fathers and mothers of their hearts' cheer. Man's mind is powerless, wisdom is silenced. Nothing can be found to stop a bacillus. It paralyzes children, the light of our lives, We await God's miracle that this should never come again.

Crowned heads and diplomats, in order to be victorious, force us to be soldiers, They drive us into battle. Young people by the millions pay their price and their flesh becomes cannon fodder. And the crippled and dead fall here and there; new lives are prepared to take their place. And in great deep graves many bodies are packed. And the rulers, the kings, play chess.

This song was written decades after the time period it references but I thought it belonged here with its predecessors.

Der milyoner fun Delancey Street

Leo Fuchs 1951

DER MILYONER FUN DELANCEY STREET

Yes, ikh bin der milyoner fun Delancey Street
Un s'iz mir gut do, dos iz nit keyn shpas,
Vayl ikh bin der milyoner fun Delancey Street
Un ikh spatsir mit Rockefeller af der gas.

Er smokt tsigarn un dem kop halt er farrisn hoykh
Un ikh gey hinter im un khap arayn dem gantsn roykh.
Ikh bin der milyoner fun Delancey Street
Un s'iz mir gut vayl ikh bin af Delancey Street.

Vos zogt ir tsu dem sutele, dem rekele, dem bloyzn?
S'kost tsvey un tsvansik dolar
un kh'hob nokh dray par hoyzn.
Ikh hob gebitn zikh in gantsn, itster bin ikh raykh
Vayl in Amerike hot zikh gechanged do mayn life.
Ikh hob itster altsding, ikh gey arum un ikh zing.

Yes, ikh bin der milyoner fun Delancey Street
Un s'iz mir gut, dos shray ikh vi se vilt.
Yes, ikh bin der milyoner fun Delancey Street
Un ikh shpatsir mikh dokh mit Gloria Vanderbilt.

Ikh zog ir,
"Let's go for a walk in park vu se blost a vintl."
Entfert zi: "Nem beser for a vok ba mir dos hintl."
Ikh bin der milyoner fun Delancey Street
Un s'iz mir gut vayl ikh bin af Delancey Street.

Yes, ikh bin der milyoner fun Delancey Street
Un s'iz mir gut do, dos iz nit keyn shpas.
Vayl ikh bin der milyoner fun Delancey Street
Un ikh spatsir mit Rockefeller af der gas.

Ir kent zikh forshteln vi mayn room iz fayn,
bakveym un groys,
Az ven di zun kumt arayn, muz ikh bald aroys.
Yes, ikh bin der milyoner fun Delancey Street
Un s'iz mir gut vayl ikh bin af Delancey Street.

Yes, I am the millionaire from Delancey Street, and I'm happy here, that's no joke, because I'm the millionaire from Delancey Street and I walk down the street with Rockefeller.

He smokes cigars and sticks his nose up in the air, and I walk behind him and inhale all the smoke. I am the millionaire from Delancey Street and I like it, because I'm on Delancey Street.

How do you like the suit, the jacket and the shirt? Cost 22 dollars and I have three more pairs of pants. I ordered it all, now I'm rich, because in America my life has changed. Now I have everything, I walk around and sing.

Yes, I am the millionaire from Delancey Street And I'm happy here, I shout it out as I please. Yes, I am the millionaire from Delancey Street, and I even walk with Gloria Vanderbilt.

I say to her, "Let's go for a walk in the park, where there's a breeze." She says: "Better you should take my little dog for a walk." I am the millionaire of Delancey Street, and I'm happy, because I'm on Delancey Street.

Yes, I am the millionaire from Delancey Street and I'm happy here, that's no joke. Because I am the millionaire from Delancey Street and I walk down the street with Rockefeller.

You can imagine my room, large, fine, and comfortable. But when the sun shines in, I must go outside. Yes, I am the millionaire from Delancey Street And I'm happy, because I'm on Delancey Street.

Mister, bay vos arbet ir?

Rubin Doctor

A nayer gezets iz yetst faran, men fregt bald vi men zet a man:
Mister, bay vos arbet ir?
Arumgeyn leydik tor men nit, men ketsht aykh on in mitn strit:
Mister, bay vos arbet ir?
Shemt aykh nit s'iz nit keyn shand, arbeter darf yetst dos land
Mister bay vos arbet ir?
Nemt dem ayzn mit der sher, makht aykh kleyder, shikh, gever, helft farnikhtn dem keyser?
Ven ir zet a man in strit, fregt im bald, fargest nor nit

Mister/missus, bay vos arbet ir? Entfert mir du glaykh geshvind.
Unkl Sem badarf aykh neytik helft im oys atsind
Shneler shneler hurry op before a policeman git aykh a hop.
Mister/missus bay vos arbet ir,
Entfert mir du glaykh geshvind.

Next door mayn shkheyne in shtub zi zitst,
A gantsn tog iz zi farputst
Missus bay vos arbet ir?
Es kumen mentshn on a shir,
Men get tsu tsvey, tsu dray, tsu fir,
Missus, bay vos arbet ir?
Ir man aleyn, er arbet nit.
Dokh lebn zey zikh fayn un git
Missus bay vos arbet ir?
Mentshn kumen mentshn geyn un zi blaybt keyn mol aleyn
ver ken zi farshteyn?
Zi geyn keynmol in strit, efsher veyst ir vos zi tit?

Missus, bay vos arbet ir? entfert mir geshvind.
Unkl Sem badarf aykh neytik zukht aykh mit likht atsind
Missus

Dort zitst a boy vos lakht un kvelt
Er lebt a tog un varft mit gelt
Mister bay vos arbet ir?
Er vatsht yeder rayt un left, er zukht tsu makhn a gesheft,
Mister bay vos arbet ir?
A partner iz er umetum a gentleman vos makht zikh frum
Mister bay vos arbet ir?
Trogt a stofpipe mit a frockcoat krikht in a fremdn pocket
zukht a vatsh un chain, a locket
ven er zitst lebn aykh zolt ir im fregn glaykh:

There's a new law now, when you see a man you ask: "Mister, what's the work you do?" You can't go around idle, you'll get nabbed in the street Don't be embarrassed, it's no shame, the land needs workers now Take the iron and the scissors, make clothes, shoes, weapons, Help annihilate the Kaiser! When you see a man in the street, ask him right off, don't forget:

Answer me right away. Uncle Sam really needs you, help him right now! Hurry hurry, hurry up, before a policeman gets you

Next door, my neighbor sits at home, all day she's dressed up Missus, what's the work you do? Men are coming endlessly, by twos, threes, fours Her husband, he doesn't work. But they live very well. Men come and go, and she is never alone, who can understand her? She never goes into the street, maybe you can guess what she does?

A boy's sitting there who laughs and beams, he lives well and throws money around He's watching everybody right and left, he's trying to do business He's a partner everywhere, a gentleman who pretends piety He wears top hat and tails, he sneaks into a stranger's pocket He seeks a watch and chain, a locket... When he sits next to you, ask him right off:

Mister Malekh ha-Moves, ikh bin busy!

by Nellie Casman 1926

100

I've written lots of songs, tunes and lyrics both I've sung for Jews and gentiles The world has my songs on records and in print I certainly didn't deserve thanks like this! It happened while I was unbelievably busy That's when the Angel of Death heard it straight from me: I'm too busy, I'm also too busy to die When death comes around, I tell him: Don't bother me!

Mr Angel of Death, I'm busy! Dying isn't easy at all. I have to go to a wedding, I have to go to a bris And I have to go dancing a little bit, too. Mr Angel of Death, I'm busy. Leave me alone, I'm getting dizzy! I'm a respectful person, I'll donate a holy book to the synagogue Mr Angel of Death, I'm busy, and that's all.

Last night I was lying in bed, very sick, Counting up how much money it was costing me. Suddenly I see the Angel of Death, he says to me: "Your name's Nellie Casman, right? Come with me." That's when I did a little thinking with my clever head How to deceive the Angel of Death, and quickly!? Pretty soon I came up with a good plan, With awe and respect this is how I answered:

If David Kessler had followed my clever plan He would still be starring in "Shloymke Charletan" If Yankev P. Adler had listened to me To this day he'd still be playing King Lear for us You're lucky, you're fortunate, my dear friends, That you came to hear Nellie Casman tonight. When - God forbid! - the Angel of Death visits you, What will you say to him? Everybody tell me!

Mr Malach Hamooves ikh bin 'busy'

Nellie Casman

Mr Malach Hamooves ikh bin 'busy'

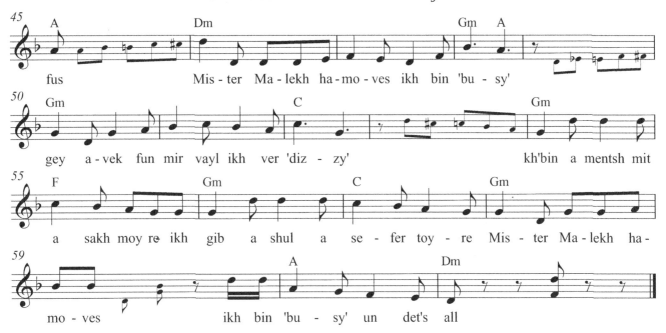

fus Mis - ter Ma - lekh ha - mo - ves ikh bin 'bu - sy'

gey a - vek fun mir vayl ikh ver 'diz - zy' kh'bin a mentsh mit

a sakh moy re ikh gib a shul a se - fer toy - re Mis - ter Ma - lekh ha -

mo - ves ikh bin 'bu - sy' un det's all

Ikh bin gelegn zeyer krank nekhtn shpet baynakht

Un gerekhent vifl gelt es hot mikh oysgebrakht

Plutsim ze ikh der malakh hamoves er shteyt un zogt tsu mir:

"Du heyst Neli Kesman, no? kum-zhe yetst mit mir"

Do hob ikh gegebn a kler mit mayn klugn kop

Vi optsunarn dem malakh hamoves oyf shnel arop?

ayngefaln iz mir bald a gutn plan

un mit moyre un "respect" hob ikh entfert dan:

Ven David Kessler volt geven gefolgt mayn klugn plan

Volt er yetst geshpilt far undz nokh "Shloymke Charlatan"

Ven Yankev P. Adler volt zikh tsugehert tsu mir

Volt er nokh haynt far undz geshpilt dem Kenig Lir

Ir zent 'lucky' ir zent gliklekh mayne libe fraynd

Vos ir zent gekumen hern Neli Kesman haynt

Ven, Got bahit, der Malakh Hamoves kumt tsu geyn tsu aykh

Vos vet ir im entfern, zogt mir ale glaykh:

די מומע גליקעלע
DIE MÜME GLÜCKELE

FROM THE PLAY:
THE WIDOW
SUCCESSFULLY PRODUCED
AT THE KALICH THEATRE N.Y.

פאן דעם לעבענספילד:
דיא אלמנה
געשפילט מיט גרוים ערפאלג
אין קאליש טהעאטר נ.י.

SONGS OF THE PLAY:
1) DIE MÜME GLÜCKELE.
2) DIE TFILLIN
3) MEN SHART GOLD IN AMERICA
4) KING SOLOMON'S SONG OF SONGS (שיר השירים)

WORDS BY
A. SCHOR

MUSIC BY
PERLMUTTER
and
WOHL

FOR
PIANO

FOR
VIOLIN.

PUBLISHED BY ~
A. TERES
MUSIC DEALER AND PUBLISHER
240½ E. HOUSTON ST., N.Y.

I knew a coarse young man, he used to be a bootblack. In playing cards and everything else you never saw such a buffoon. But suddenly he's a modern fellow, people compliment him quite a bit. He wants to know about everything and be a bigshot. So we're all asking ourselves, how'd he get to be such a nabob? The answer is: his money.

Because Lady Luck favors him a bit. She sits comfortably on both sides of this exemplary guy. As soon as Lady Luck smiles on you, you may be an oaf, a nothing, suddenly you're a fine fellow.

I knew two maidens here, they spent time together. One was beautiful, the second ugly as the night. Both went out with the same young man. All three loved each other in a group. He hung around with the pretty one but he married the ugly one. I was almost crazy. My friend said in a quiet moment: she has money, brother, that's what I want.

I knew a young man who took a rich girl. He got the dowry and death swept her away. Barely is the 30 day mourning period over when he gets married again and receives a fresh dowry from the second wife, that harridan. But hear what happened: The second is already lying in the earth, too, and my boy now is thinking about a third.

Die Mieme Glikale.

Sung by Mr. BERNSTEIN.

Words by A. SCHOR.
Music by PERLMUTTER & WOHL.

Con spirito. *Lively.*

Moderato.

Ich hob ge-kent a gro-ben jing a shtie vel pit-zer a mul ge ven vus in der kurt in chitz al ding a sa mien letz hot men nit ge sehn nor pli tzem hebt er un gur datsh zu shmiesen in men sugt him shon nuch shvo-chim fin al-le zu-res vill er shon vi-sen

2.

Ich hob gekent du Meidlech zwei
Zusamen hoben sei ferbracht
Gevehn is eine shehn fin sei
Die zweite Miess vie die Nacht
Mit ein Jingen Man senin beide gegangen
In geliebt sich in Chawriesse
Noch der shehner hot er sich Pushit gehangen
Nor chassene gehat mit der Miesse

Ich bin gebliben nor asoj vie dill
Erklert mir mein freind in der Still
Sie hot geld Brieder duss vus ich vill.

CHORUS:

3.

Ich hob gekent a Jungen Man
Wus hot genimen a Reiche Majd
Bekimen hot er dem Nadan
In aveg gechapt hot sie der tojt

Kaum is er die Shlojshim iber gekimen
Stelt er shojn a Naje Chipe
Er hot a frishen Nadan genimen
Bei dem zweiten weib der klipe
Nor Hert vus hot getrofen Hert
Die zweite ligt shojn auch in der Erd
In auf a Dritter mein Bucher jezt klehrt

CHORUS:

NOCH-A-BISEL-EPES NOCH

Words by L. Gilrod - Music by M. J. Rubinsteirt.

נאָך אַ ביסעלע עפּעס נאָך

Ikh bin a groyser freser, keyn zakh lib ikh nit beser
Vi nor kayen, esn, fresn fil oy oy oy
Ir megt fun mir lakhn, nor git mir gute zakhn,
Plenti nashn, ot dos vos ikh vil.
Mer ikh es un mer ikh trinkt on shir
Imer mer, imer glust zikh mir,

Oy, vey,
epes nokh un epes nokh un nokh nokh nokh
Un nokh a steak un nokh a cake un nokh nokh nokh
Nokh a yakhl arayn in baykhl, nokh a chicken arayn tsurikn,
Nokh, nokh oy un epes nokh

2
Ot voyn ikh bay a mises, tsu fres ikh zi af 'pieces'
Far mir tsu kokhn hot zi shoyn mer keyn koyekh
Vayl ikh hob zi farmutshet, der man, er shrayt un kvitshet,
Ikh fres af ales vos zi kokht
Der man muz in restorant esn geyn
Vayl dem gantsn 'sopper' git zi mir aleyn

Oy vey
Epes nokh un epes nokh un nokh nokh nokh
Nokh a bisl arayn in shisl un nokh nokh nokh
Nokh a kheyn'dl un nokh a beyndl, nokh a bulke un nokh a pulke
Un nokh, nokh, un epes nokh...

Ikh gey mir in theater un ze dos zelbe vayter
Mer ikh ze, als mer iz mayn bager
Derze ikh a sheyn meydl mit a 'fency' kleydl,
Nemt zi tantsn, shray ikh - ikh vil mer!
Ikh aplodir kumt zi vider aroys
Fangt zi on tsu tantsn, shray ikh oys:

Oy vey
Epes nokh un epes nokh un nokh nokh nokh
Genendel tsayg dos zakn bendel nokh nokh nokh
Nokh a dreydl gib zikh, meydl, nokh a bisl hoyb di fisl, un nokh, nokh oy un epes nokh

Only on the sheet music: Koym ze ikh mamalige, ver ikh shir meshige grashe tzeskarants lakh fertzig toyznt shtik dos es ikh gor on shpasn, dan glaykh ikh tsu farbaysn dray fir hering mit a pompanik Far tsushpayz glaykh ikh golash mit a steak A halbe katshke puding mit cheesecakez

I'm a big eater, there's nothing I love more than chewing, eating, gorging a lot, oy oy! You can laugh at me, but give me good things, Plenty to snack on, that's what I want. I eat more, I drink more, endlessly, Always more, I always desire more.

Oy vey! A little more and more and more more more. Another steak, another cake, and more more more. Another broth into my belly, another chicken to shove in, More, more, and a little more.

I live with a landlady here, I eat her to pieces, She doesn't have the strength to cook for me any more. Because I exhausted her, her man cries and shrieks. I gobble down everything she cooks. Her husband has to go to a restaurant to eat Because she gives the whole supper just to me.

Oy vey! A little more and more and more more more A little more in the bowl, more more more A little more flirting, some more "benefits" Another dinner roll, another drumstick, More, more, oy, and a little more.

I go to the theater and it's more of the same: The more I see, the more I want. I catch sight of a pretty girl in a fancy dress, She starts dancing, I shout - I want more! I applaud, she comes out again, She starts dancing, I shout :

Oy vey! A little more and more and more more more! Genendl, show your garter! (ribbons on your socks) Twirl again, girl, lift your leg! More, more, oy! and a little more...

Only on the sheet music: Koym ze ikh mamalige, ver ikh shir meshige grashe tzeskarants lakh fertzig toyznt shtik dos es ikh gor on shpasn, dan glaykh ikh tsu farbaysn dray fir hering mit a pompanik Far tsushpayz glaykh ikh golash mit a steak A halbe katshke puding mit cheesecake

I go crazy when I see mamalige [other food] 40,000 pieces, I eat them (no joke) then three or four herring with [other food] goulash, steak, half a duck, pudding, and cheesecake.

NOCH A BISEL IN ESPES NOCH

Words by
L. GILROD.

Music by
M. J. RUBINSTEIN.

Itzik

Ven Itske's do ge-ku-men hot er zikh bald ge-nu-men
Nit bet-n lozt zikh Its-ke un nemt zikh glaykh tsum shmit-shik un

lern-en shpil-n fid-l un nit mer Yetst halt er in eyn
heybt on fid-len mit zayn gants-n koyekh Di mis-sus zitst un

skri-pn un voynt by So-re Tsip-n im her-n shpil-n
freyt zikh der spo-dik bay ir dreyt-zikh zi heybt on tants-n

iz nor ir ba-ger. Koym geyt ir man nor fun der shtub a-roys
shpring-en in der hoykh Plut-sim kumt ir man a-rayn tsu geyn

khapt zi on Its-ken un shrayt tsu im oys oy vey!
Treft It-sik-n fid-len un mit dem shmit-shik shteyn

It-sik It-sik nem dayn shmit-shik shpil shpil shpil Nem dem fid-l
muf muf muf Hit dir di bey-ner

shpil a lid-l shpil shpil shpil a ko-zat-ske un a khats-ke
shey-gets ey-ner muf muf muf Far-pak dem shmit-shik shpil nit It-sik

shpil zhe It-zik mit dayn shmit-shik shpil shpil shpil zhe It-zik shpil
Stop shoyn skrip-n So-re Tsip-n muf muf muf zhe It-zik muf

Ven Itske iz do gekumen hot er zikh bald genumen
Lernen shpiln fidl un nit mer
Yestst halt er in eyn skripn un voynt by Sore Tsipn
Im hern shpiln iz nor ir bager
Koym geyt ir man nor fun der shtib aroys
Khapt zi on Itsken un shrayt tsu im oys! Oy vey!

Itsik Itsik nem dayn shmitshik shpil shpil shpil
Nem dem fidl shpil a lidl shpil shpil shpil
A kozatske un a khatske shpil zhe Itsik mit dayn shmitshik
Shpil shpil shpil zhe Itsik, shpil!

Nit betn lozt zikh Itsik un nemt zikh glaykh tsum shmitshik
Un heybt on fidlen mit zayn gantsn koyekh
Di missus zitst un freyt zikh, der spodik bay ir dreyt zikh
Zi heyb on tantsn shpringen in der hoykh
Plutsim kumt ir man arayn tsu geyn
Treft Itsikn fidlen un mit dem shmitshik shteyn oy vey!

Itsik Itsik nem dem shmitshik, muf muf muf
Hit dir di beyner sheygets eyner muf muf muf
Farpak dem shmitshik shpil nit Itsik
Stop shoyn skripn Sore Tsipn
Muf muf muf zhe Itsik muf

Ayngepakt hot Itsik dem fidl mit zayn shmitshik
Un arayngemuft glaykh tsu der missus vint
Kumt plutsim dort tsu krikhn ganovim un zey zikhn
Der shmitshik hobn zey bay im fardint
Yetst shteyt di missus un zi kukt im on
"Vos kenstu," shrayt zi, "on a shmitshik ton?" Oy vey!

Itsik Itsik zikh dem shmitshik zukh zukh zukh
Vos kenstu toygn on dem boygn, zukh zukh zukh
Loyf geshvinder zikh atsinder
A gutn shmitshik far dir Itsik
Loyf loyf loyf zhe Itsik loyf

Avek is bald di Itsik gekoyft a nayem shmitshik
Un aheym gelofn mit im iz er geshvind
"Ikh hob," shrayt er atsinder, "a shmitshik gor a vinder!"
Un heybt on fidlen bay der missus vind
Di missus tantst far freyd poshet zi kvelt,
"Dayn shmitshik," shrayt zi, "iz vert milionen gelt!" Oy vey!

Itsik Itsik host dem shmitshik shpil shpil shpil
Farlir keyn tsayt nit shpil un reyd git shpil shpil shpil
Ikh fil gezunter ven du shpilst unter
Liber Itsik mit dayn shmitshik
Shpil shpil shpil zhe Itzik shpil

When little Itsik got here, he took to learning the fiddle, nothing more. Now he's always fiddling and lives at Sore Tsipn's place. All she desires is to hear him play. As soon as her man leaves the house she grabs Itsik and shouts to him, oy vey!

Itsik, Itsik, pick up your bow, play play play. Take your fiddle, play a little tune, play play play. A kozatske and a khatske, play with your bow, Itsik, play, play, play Itzik, play!

Itzik didn't have to be begged, he took up his bow immediately and began fiddling with all his strength. His landlady sits and enjoys herself, her hat twirls, she begins dancing, jumping up high... Suddenly her husband comes in, he finds Itsik fiddling there with his bow, oy!

Itsik Itsik pick up your bow and move, move, move. Watch out for broken bones, you scalawag! Move, move, move. Pack up your bow, don't play any more, Itzik, stop fiddling Sore Tsipn. Move, move, move, Itzik, move!

Itsik packed up his fiddle and bow and moved right into the landlady's. Suddenly thieves come there and they're looking around. They got his bow, now the landlady's standing and looking at him: "What can you do without a bow?" she shouts. Oy vey!

Itsik Itsik look for your bow, look look look. What good are you without the bow? Look look look Run quickly, look for a good bow right now, Itsik Run run run Itsik run.

So Itsik is away quickly to buy a new bow and he runs home quickly with it. "I have," he shouts now, "a wonderful bow!" And he begins fiddling by the landlady's. The landlady dances for joy, she's simply beaming, "Your bow," she cries, "is worth a million dollars!" Oy vey!

Itsik Itsik, you have the bow, play play play. Don't waste time, play and talk well, play play play. I feel more healthy when you play with your bow, dear Itsik, Play play play Itzik, play!

די אָפּגענאַרטע וועלט

(ווערטער און מוזיק פון ש. פריזאַמענט. פון הערש בראָדערס
(הערשל בדחן) רעפּערטואַר)

114

Di opgenarte velt

Repertoire of Hersh Broder (Hershl Badkhn)

Sh. Prizament

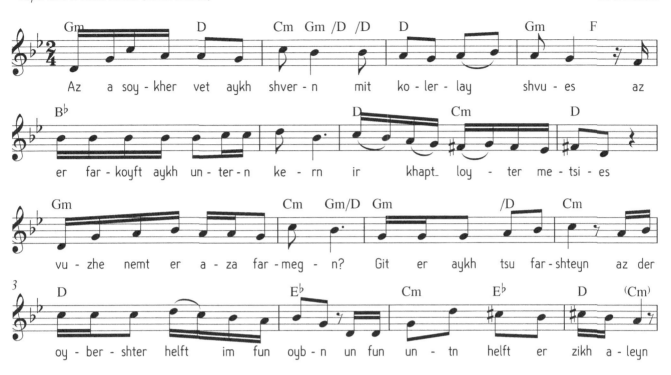

Az a soy-kher vet aykh shver-n mit ko-ler-lay shvu-es az

er far-koyft aykh un-ter-n ke-rn ir khapt loy-ter me-tsi-es

vu-zhe nemt er a-za far-meg-n? Git er aykh tsu far-shteyn az der

oy-ber-shter helft im fun oyb-n un fun un-tn helft er zikh a-leyn

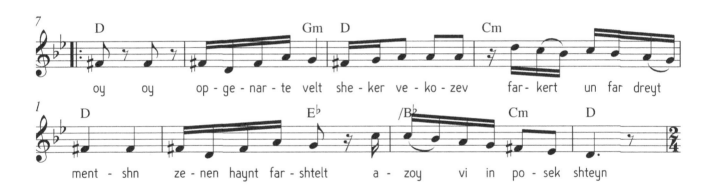

oy oy op-ge-nar-te velt she-ker ve-ko-zev far-kert un far dreyt

ment-shn ze-nen haynt far-shtelt a-zoy vi in po-sek shteyn

Az a soykher vet aykh shvern
mit kolerlay shvues
az er farkoyft aykh untern kern
ir khapt loyter metsies
vuzhe nemt er aza farmegn?
Git er aykh tsu farshteyn
az der oybershter helft im fun oybn
un fun untn helft er zikh aleyn

oy oy opgenarte velt
sheker vekozev farkert un fardreyt
mentshn zenen haynt farshtelt
azoy vi in posek shteyn

Ven Yoysef iz geven in mitsrayim
Vos hot mit im getrofn?
Putifers vayb hot im arumgenumen
Hot er zikh oysgerisn un antlofn
Ober hayntike besmedrish bokhurim
Tsi Yoysef, tsi Zorekh, tsi Borukh
Az er zet durkhn fentster geyn a bsule
Fargesn er in shulkhan arukh

Khane-Beyle shteyt un taynet
Mit a bokher fun der yeshive
Er redt fun Got un fun tsitsis
Un zi makht mines vi a naive
Plutsim hot der bokher, nisht vilndik,
Ongerirt di hant bay Khane-Beyle
Zi shrayt "On hent, yungerman!"
A kush iz epes andersh. Nu, meyle!

When a merchant swears to you up and down That he's selling below cost and everything is a great bargain Where is he making his money? He'll tell you: "God helps from above, and down here, I do it all himself."

Oy, the deluded world. Nothing but lies, upside down and sideways. People are posers these days, just as it's written in Scripture

When Joseph was in Israel what happened to him? Potipher's wife grabbed him but he tore away from her and ran! But schoolboys today, be it Joseph, Zorekh, or Barukh When he looks out the window and sees a girl he forgets The Code of Jewish Law

Khana-Beyle stands and argues with a boy from the yeshiva He talks about God and religious garb She feigns a naive expression Suddenly the boy, unintentionally, touches her hand She yells, "hands off, young man!" A kiss, though, that's something different. What can you do?

Shabes koydesh p1

A gantse vokh iz dokh dos yidele farshmakht.
Er loyft un koyft un flit un tit bay tog un bay nakht
Er zorgt un borgt un arbet shver un plogt zikh mitn toyt
tsulib dem trukenem shtikele broyt
Er laydet tsores un yesurim on a tsol
dos vayb un kinder hungern ale mol
Me horevet me arbet in dayges fil me shvimt biz der
shabes koydesh kimt.

Dan zetst men zikh gants frish baym sheyn gedekte tish
mit kiddish un mit khale un mit fish!

Shabes koydesh baym yidele iz dos tayerste sudele
freylekh zingt er dos lidele fun kol mekadesh shvii

Dos shabes koydesh nigele mit dem lokshn kigele An est
a trinkele in yeder vinkele
Shpiglt zikh der liber shabes koydesh

Di bentsh likht brenen in di laykhter glantsn sheyn, Di
shabes kale shvebt arum fil prakht un kheyn
Dos yidele bagrist zi un empfangt zi mit fil freyd er nemt
zi uf mit zise reyd
Lekha dodi lekratkala zingt er ir fargest zikh in di tsores
un di dayges fun frier
Dos vayb un kinder shabesdik un lebedik geshtimt ven
der shabes koydesh kumt
Dan zetst men zikh gants frish tsum sheyn gedekte tish
mit kiddish un mit khale un mit fish!

The whole week long the Jew is tired. He runs and buys and flies and works day and night, he worries and borrows and works hard and is plagued onto death just to get a dry bit of bread.

He suffers endless worries and miseries. His wife and children are always hungry. One slaves away in poverty, one swims in it until the holy Sabbath comes.

Then one sits down, refreshed, by the beautifully bedecked table with the kiddesh, with challah, with fish.

Because the holy Sabbath is the dearest feast for the Jew. He sings the song happily: "Who duly keeps the Sabbath..."

The holy Sabbath song, and the noodle pudding, a candelabra, a little drink, and the dear holy Sabbath sparkles in every corner.

The Sabbath candles burn and the candlesticks shine. The Sabbath bride hovers, so beautiful and charming. The Jew greets her, welcomes her so happily. He brings her in with sweet speech.

He sings "Let's go, my beloved, to meet the bride" to her. He forgets the troubles and the poverty of before. His wife and children are in a happy Sabbath mood when the holy Sabbath comes.

Shtek Arayn

vamp is first two bars of the chorus

Ve - men iz den nisht ba - kant der min - heg af der gantser velt   tsu ge - bn shten - dik dir di hant

vayl es kost dokh nisht keyn gelt   kurts tsi iz der oy - lem greyt dir zog - n 'for ge - zun - ter - heyt!'

un bay key - nem nisht ge - klert men zogt zikh ot vos hert: Shtek a - rayn   zay nit keyn

frey - er   Shtek a - rayn   es kost nit tay - er   U - me - tum af

a - le veg - n trogt mit dir di hent ant - keg - n sho - lem   a - ley - khem   bri - der shtek a - rayn
a la - pe shtek a - rayn

Mayn kozin Itzik hot a vaybl, zeyer a sheyne gur a prakht

Kumt zayn fraynt arayn in shtub an umglik treft nishto gedakht

Antlofn mitn fraynt iz zi, un Itzik fartsveyflt veyst nit vi

Treft im amol zayn fraynt in gas un zugt tsu em mit shpas...

Shtek arayn zay nit keyn frayer. Shtek arayn es kost nit tayer

Du darfst zikh far mir gornisht feyln, me kon es zikh mit dir tsuteyln

Shulem, aleykhem, Itzik shtek arayn.

Shtek arayn, zay nit keyn frayer. Shtek arayn, es kost nit tayer.

Zi vet far beydn vashn, kokhn, dir af shabes, mir in d'vokhn

Shulem, aleykhem, Itzik shtek arayn

Mit mayn vaybl bin ikh gegangen in teater yene nakht

Geyt farbay a sheyne vaybl, koketirt, tsu mir gelakht

Geyt zi redn bloyz a vort, burtshet shoyn mayn vaybl dort

Zi lozt arop af mir a nuz un freykt mikh vus iz dus?   Zog ikh:

Shtek arayn, zay nit keyn frayer. Shtek arayn, es kost nit tayer.

Kokht zikh nisht es iz umzist vayl zi vil visn ver di bist.

Shulem aleykhem, a lape shtek arayn

Who doesn't know the whole world's custom: Always to give your hand, because it doesn't cost a cent Right away people are ready to wish you a safe journey And when you return, this is what you'll hear:

Give it here, don't be a chump. Give it here, it doesn't cost anything. Everywhere, on all paths, folks are ready to give you a hand. "Greetings, brothers, put 'er there." (second time: put out your paw)

My cousin Itzik has a really pretty wife His friend comes into the house, something unfortunate happens (let it not happen to us) She runs away with the friend! And Itzik, depressed, doesn't know where. His friend runs into him in the street and says jokingly:

Put 'er there, don't be a chump. Put 'er there, it doesn't cost anything! You won't miss out on my account, we can share her Hi, Itzik, put 'er there. Put 'er there, don't be a chump. Put 'er there, it doesn't cost anything She can wash and cook for both of us - you on the Sabbath, me during the week. Greetings, Itzik, put 'er there.

I went to the theater with my wife the other night. A pretty woman walked by, she flirted, she laughed with me She goes to say just a word, my wife is already grumbling She looks down her nose at me and asks: what's going on?

I say: come on, don't be a chump. Come on, it doesn't cost anything Don't blow a gasket, there's no point, she wants to get to know you

The Great Hit of Thomashefsky's "People's Theatre"

DAS·PINTELE·YUD

דאם פינטעלע יוד

SUNG BY

MASTER THOMASHEFSKY

WORDS BY L. GILROD

composed and arranged
BY

·· PERLMUTTER & WOHL ··

1. Dos Pintele Yud.   דאם פינטעלע יוד. .1
2. Bar-Mitzvah March   בר־מצוה מארטש. .2
3. Yisrolik in Sein Eigen Land.   ישראליק אין זיין אייגען לאנד. .3
4. Seit Klug un Shtoist Sich On.   זייט קלוג אן שטויסם זיך אן. .4
5. Menshele meinst Du west Eibig Leben.   מענשעלע מיינסט דו וועסט אייביג לעבען. .5
6. Oi! s'is mir wohl, Oi! s'is Mir Gut.   אוי! ס'איז מיר וואויל, אוי! ס'איז מיר גוט. .6

טהרי טשירם פאר יענקי דודל. :טריטצעם
7. Three Cheers for Yankee Doodle.

Piano
each
50

Violin
complete
75¢

HEBREW PUBLISHING CO.
50-52 ELDRIDGE STREET   NEW YORK
COPYRIGHT 1909.

122

Shtoyst zikh on

123

Di mode fun der letster tsayt tsu zogn bin ikh aykh
do oysn
Es git fil zakhn haynt bay layt vos me darf zikh aleyn
oyf zey shtoysn
A moyd, tsum bayshpil, zet ir arumgeyn shpatsirn
mit fil yungelayt
Un vos zi zukht darft ir zikh onshtoysn un visn
shoyn vos dos badayt
Vos zi zukht, vos ir felt, volt ikh aykh do gants ofn
dertseylt

Nor shtoyst zikh on, zayt klug un shtoyst zikh on
Azelkhe zakhn zaynen gants laykht tsum farshteyn
Klert nit keyn sakh, dos iz a klore zakh,
Zayt nit keyn goylem, shtoyst zikh on aleyn

A raykher man hot lib zayn froy, far libe falt er far ir
koyrim
Nor zi iz, nebekh, krank azoy, men halt in eyn rufn
doktoyrim.
Ambestn ven dem man nor farglust zikh tsu redn
mit zayn froy a vort,
Iz gor di tir fun tsimer farshlosn, der yuntgitshker
doktor iz dort.
Af vos zi krenkt, un vos ir felt, volt ikh aykh do gants
ofn dertseylt

Nor shtoyst zikh on, zayt klug un shtoyst zikh on,
Azelkhe zakhn zaynen gants laykht tsum farshteyn.
S'a klore zakh, a doktor helft a sakh,
Zayt nit keyn yoldes, shtoist zikh on aleyn.

I'm going to tell you about how things are nowadays. A lot of things people are doing today, you ought to be able to figure them out yourself. A girl, for example, you see her walking around with a lot of young guys, and what she's looking for, you yourself can guess, and know what it means. What she's looking for, what she's lacking, I'd tell you about it here:

But figure it out yourself, be smart and figure it out, such things are easy to understand. Don't think about it, it's pretty clear. Don't be a dummy, figure it out yourself.

A rich man loves his wife, he prostrates himself with adoration. But she, poor thing, is sick! Doctors are constantly being summoned. Especially when the husband just wants a word with his wife, the door is locked! The new young doctor is with her... What's making her sick, what she's lacking, I could explain to you here...

But figure it out yourself, be smart and figure it out, Such things are easy to understand. It's clear! A doctor is a lot of help! Don't be chumps, figure it out yourself.

צרות איז קיין

דאגה ניט

פון דער אפערא יציאת מצרים

ZORES IS KAIN DAIGE NIT

From YZIAS MIZRAJUM

Words by Prof. HOROWITZ **Music by PERLMUTTER and WOHL**

PUBLISHED BY

THE HEBREW PUBLISHING CO.

50-52 Eldridge Str., New York

Tsores iz keyn dayge nit

Mayns a fraynd hot mir der - tseylt
az vos er darf rak im felt es geyt im in zayn leb - n nit git
un vos der darf hot er nit. Er hot keyn ru er hot keyn freyd er
hot keyn shu er hot keyn kleyd er hot keyn leb - n er hot keyn toyt er
hot keyn heym er hot keyn broyt. Er hot keyn vayb er hot keyn kind. Er
hot keyn maz - l er hot keyn ge - zint. er hot keyn ko - ved, er hot keyn gelt, er
hot nit di, nit ye - ne velt! Dokh vet ir zen ye - der kap - tsn shten - dik lakht un kvelt un iz
to - mid frey - lekh af ye - dn shrit un trit. Ikh, zogt er, hob in d'rerd a - fi - le di
gan - tse velt vayl ikh veys nor hu - lye kap - tsn tso - res iz keyn day - ge nit.

Mayns a fraynd hot mir dertseylt az vos er darf rak im felt
Es geyt im in zayn lebn nit git un vos der darf hot er nit.
Er hot keyn ru er hot keyn freyd er hot keyn shu er hot keyn kleyd
Er hot keyn lebn er hot keyn toyt er hot keyn heym er hot keyn broyt.
Er hot keyn vayb er hot keyn kind. Er hot keyn mazl er hot keyn gezint.
Er hot keyn koved, er hot keyn gelt, er hot nit di, nit yene velt!

Dokh vet ir zen yeder kaptsn shtendik lakht un kvelt
Un iz tomid freylekh af yedn shrit un trit.
Ikh, zogt er, hob in d'rerd afile di gantse velt
Vayl ikh veys nor hulye kaptsn tsores iz keyn dayge nit.

Kumt tsum oreman in shtib iz vist un ler vi in a grib
Er firt zeyer a groyshartik hoyz nor a shtikl broyt felt im oys
Er hot keyn tir er hot keyn dakh er hot keyn bet er hot keyn zakh
Er hot keyn zeyger er hot keyn shpigl er hot keyn kishen er hot keyn shpigl
Er hot keyn khale er hot keyn tish er hot keyn fleysh er hot keyn fish
er hot keyn fefer er hot keyn zalts, er hot keyn puter er hot keyn shmalts.

Troubles are nothing to worry about

A friend of mine told me he lacked everything he should have
Things aren't going well in his life, and he doesn't have what he needs.
He has no peace, he has no happiness, he has no shoes, he has no clothes.
He has no life, he has no death, he has no home, he has no bread.
He has no wife, he has no child, he has no luck, he has no health.
He has no honor, he has no money, he doesn't have this world or the world to come.

*Naturally, you'll see every pauper always laughing and delighted, and he's always
happy at every turn. He says "To hell with the whole world, because I go by 'Live it
up, pauper, troubles are nothing to worry about!'"*

Come to a poor man's house, it's as empty as the grave
It's a bighearted place, but he doesn't have even a bit of bread.
He has no door, he has no roof, he has no bed, he has nothing.
He has no clock, he has no mirror, he has no pillows, he has no cradle.
He has no challah, he has no table, he has no meat, he has no fish.
He has no pepper, he has no salt, he has no butter, he has no chicken fat.

וואַרעניקעס

מיט גריבען

פון צרות פון קינדער

אראַנזשירט פון לואים פריעדזעל.

Warenikes mit Griben

FUN ZORES FUN KINDER
Music by L. FRIEDSELL

PUBLISHED BY

HEBREW PUBLISHING CO.
50-52 ELDRIDGE STR., NEW YORK

Tseytele iz a voyle. Varenikes mit gribn.
Zaytzhe kinder nit keyn foyle. Varenikes mit gribn
Tseytele iz a negide. Varenikes mit gribn
Makht zi far undz a side. Varenikes mit gribn.
Tseytele git ven men bet varenikes mit gribn.

Tomid bay ir iz ongegreyt varenikes mit gribn.
Shabes oykh in mitn der vokh varenikes mit gribn.
Halbe nakht krigt ir nokh varenikes mit gribn.
Ver iz aza berye tsu makhn git varenikes mit gribn?

Keyner in shtetl makht azoy nit varenikes mit gribn.
Lomir ale esn mit apetit varenikes mit gribn.
Nokh a bisl bronfn farbayst men mit Varenikes mit gribn
Derfar oy derfar oy vey vey
Kumt ale kumt ale lomir geyen shnel a tentsl shnel.

Tseytele's a fine one, varenikes with gribn
Kids, don't be lazy. Tseytele's a rich woman.
She makes us a feast. When you ask, she gives you varenikes with gribn.

She's always got varenikes with gribn prepared.
Shabes, also the middle of teh week.
You can still get them at night. Who's as good as she is at making them?

Nobody in town makes such good varenikes with gribn.
Let's all eat with appetite.
A little more whiskey accompanied by varenikes with gribn.
So, oy vey, come everybody, let's go dance.

Varenikes are dumplings and gribn (griwen) are chicken fat
cracklings.

Varenikes mit gribn

Louis Friedsell

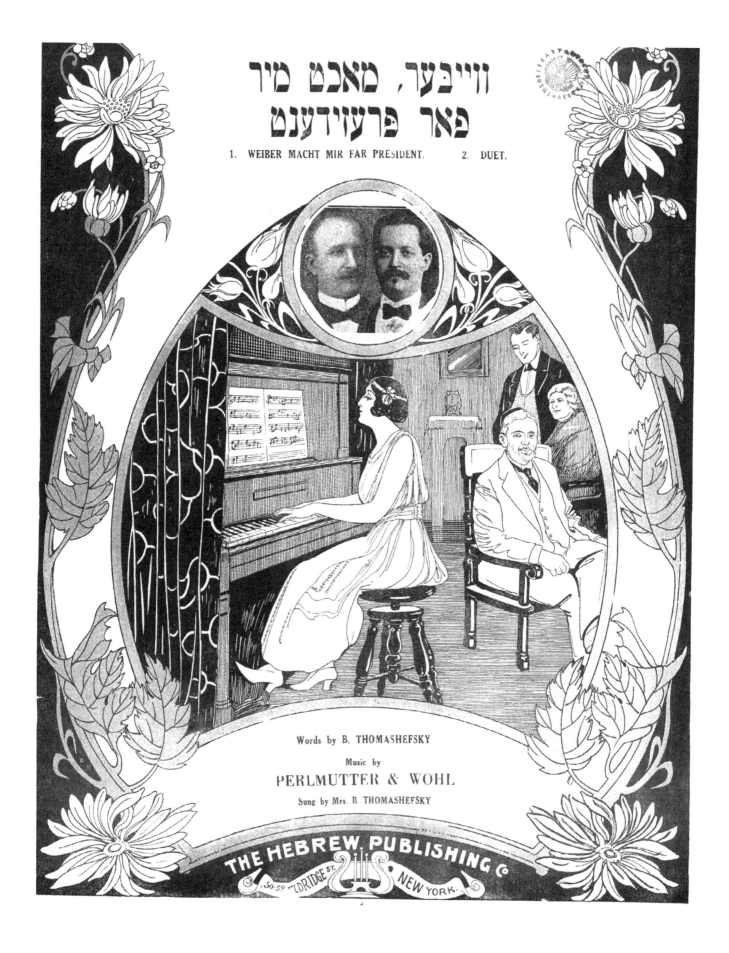

וייבער, מאכט מיר פאר פרעזידענט

1. WEIBER MACHT MIR FAR PRESIDENT.   2. DUET.

Words by B. THOMASHEFSKY

Music by

PERLMUTTER & WOHL

Sung by Mrs. B. THOMASHEFSKY

THE HEBREW PUBLISHING Co.
50-59 ELDRIDGE ST., NEW YORK.

Oy vayber, vayber, vayber! Hert vos ikh zog aykh, vayber!
Oy vayber, vayber, vayber! Nemt aykh tsuzamen, vayber!
A meeting lomir, vayber, makhn in dem shensten hall,
Di mener megn fun unz lakhn, lakhn mit der gal.
Mir, vayber, muzn protestirn, s'geyt nit vayter mer.
Nor bay di noz di mener firn, vayber, s'iz nit shver.

Nemt aykh tsuzamen, vayber! Makht mikh far a prezident!
Vet ir zen, vayber, vi mir haltn di mener in di hent.

Oy vayber, vayber, vayber! Zayt nit keyn katshkes, vayber!
Oy vayber, vayber, vayber! Nor makht a meeting, vayber,
Ikh vart oykh in Eldridge Street, in hall bay Mr. Smalle.
Haynt nemt a sof, es geyt mer nit. Nemt aykh tsuzamen ale!
Mir, vayber, veln zikh aynsparn, vayzn mener gut
Az vayber ken men eyn mol naren, tsvey mol geyt es nit!

Oy vayber, vayber, vayber! Kokht nit keyn dinner, vayber!
Oy vayber, vayber, vayber! Fort nit in country, vayber!
Ven es kumt der liber zumer, di zun git nor a brih,
Farshlist ir shoyn ayer tsimer, un loyft in der country!
Oy di mener, di mamzirim, hoylen tog un nakht,
Un fraytig punkt vi di khazeyrim hot zey di train gebrakht.

Oy vayber, vayber, vayber! Hot nit keyn kinder, vayber!
Oy vayber, vayber, vayber! Gvald, zayt nit keyn vayber!
Zoln di mener diapers vashen, hert ir a geshrey,
Lost zey fun di teplekh nashen, un kinder hobn zoln zey.
Lomir zey lozn bargains ketshen in Wanamaker's store,
Un zol zey nor di corset kvetshen khotsh tsvey mol a yor.

Oy women, women, women! Listen to me, women! Oy women, women, women! Get it together, women! We'll hold a meeting in the finest hall. The men may laugh at us, laugh with gall. Women, we must protest! Things can't go on this way. But it's not hard, women, to lead men by the nose.

Get together, women! Make me your president! Women, you'll see how we hold the men in our hands.

Oy women, women, women! Don't be silly geese, women! Oy women, women, women! Just hold a meeting, women, I'll meet you on Eldridge Street at Mr. Smalle's hall. It ends today, things can't go on. All of you, get together! Women, we won't budge, we'll teach these men that you can fool a women once, but never twice!

Oy women, women, women! Don't cook dinner, women! Oy women, women, women! Don't go to the country, women! Each year, when summer comes the sun gives us nothing but a burn, and you close up your place and run to the country. Oy, the men, those bastards, carry on day and night, then Friday the train delivers them as scheduled, like a load of hogs.

Oy women, women, women! Don't have children, women! Oy women, women, women! Oy, just don't be women! Let the men wash the diapers and you'll hear a great uproar. Let them fix the food and bear the children. Let them chase down bargains at Wanamaker's! And let them squeeze into corsets at least twice a year!

Weiber macht mich far President.

Words by B. THOMASHEFSKY.

Gesungen bei Madam Besi Thomashefsky.

Music by PERLMUTTER and WOHL.

bei die nez die | me ner fih ren | va ber siz nit | shver nemt

CHORUS.

eich zu za men | va ber macht mich | far a pre zi dent | vet ihr zehn va ber

to Coda 1 | 2 | CODA.

vie mir hal ten | di me ner in die | hent nemt | hent | D.S. | hent

2.

Oi weiber, weiber, weiber,
Seit nit kein katshkes weiber,
Oi weiber, weiber, weiber,
Nur macht a meeting, weiber.
Ich wart auch in Eldridge Street
In Hall, bei Mr. Smalle.
Heint nemt a sof, es geht mehr nit
Nemt eich zusammen alle.
Mir weiber welen sich einsparen
Weisen mener gut
As weiber ken men ein mol naren,
Zwei mol geht es nit.

CHORUS.

3.

Oi weiber, weiber, weiber,
Kocht nit kein dinner weiber,
Oi weiber, weiber, weiber,
Fort nit in country, weiber.
Wen es kimt der lieber simmer
Die sin git nor a brih
Verslist ihr schon eiere zimmer
Un lauft in der country.
Oi die mener die mamseirim
Hillien tog un nacht
Un Freitag pinkt wie die chaseirim,
Hot sei die trein gebracht.

CHORUS.

4.

Oi weiber, weiber, weiber,
Hot nit kein kinder weiber,
Oi weiber, weiber, weiber,
Gewald seit nit kein weiber.
Solen die mener deipers washen
Hert ihr a geshrei
Lost sei von die teplech nashen
Un kinder hoben solen sei.
Lomir sei losen bargains ketshen
In Wanamaker's store
Un sol sei nur der corset kwetshen
Chotsh zwei mol a johr.

CHORUS.

English Wording by
ISIDORE ABRAMSON.

Weiber. 2.

SUCCESSFUL SONGS FROM PROF. HOROWITZ'S
LODGE PRESIDENT

235511
16

דער לארזשען
פרעזידענט

COMPOSED BY

PERLMUTTER AND WOHL

WORDS BY
A. SCHORR

1. Ven Ich Sol Veren President. . . . 40
2. Liebesduett. 40

Theodore Lohr,
286 GRAND ST.
NEW YORK

Ven ikh zol vern President

Ikh bin a boy mit fil talent
vi mayn tatenyu er zol zikh mien.
Ven ikh zol vern President
volt ikh zeyer fil ufgetin.
In fil gezetse vi mir shaynt
geendert mit mayn fuler kraft
Kapital un arbet vot ikh fareynt
Un Sunday law gor opgeshaft.
Trinken zol a yeder fray.
Un poker shpiln say vi say.

Es volt gevezn a mekhaye men volt gelebt un gelakht
In a Konstitushen gor a naye volt ikh mir aleyn gemakht.
A yeder volt geven tsufridn Di yenkis un oykh di yidn
Oysfirn ales volt ikh gekent ven ikh zol vern President

Avek gemuft vel ikh Sing-Sing
In der 5th Ave ibergefirt.
Un Allen Street volt ikh zeyer gring
Vi a mol sheyn oysgetsirt
Di Politician dort bazetst
Tsu dem volt ikh nor geshtrebt
Un ikh volt zey ale yo, biz tsu letst
A Union Lebel ufgeklebt
Un di ale bloye rek
Volt ikh gegebn di sek.

Milkhome volt ikh bald derklert
Zikh tsu shlogn nor mit dem katsap
Un im bagrobn tif in der erd
Volt ikh mitn erstn klap
Mit Japan mir eyn hand gemakht
Un im onlernen git dos mol
Un geharget volt ikh bald nokh der shlakht
Von Plehve ot dem soyne yisroel
Gefreyt volt ikh mikh dan oykh zeyer
Mit der mapole fun dem rusishen ber

*I'm a boy with lots of talent, as
my father raised me. If I became
President I'd get a lot done. In a
lot of laws, you understand, I'd
change things with my full strength.
I would unite capital and labor,
abolish the Blue Laws, everybody
could drink freely and play poker as
they pleased.*

*It would be a wonder, people
would live well and laugh. I myself
would create a new Constitution.
Everybody would be happy, the
Yankees and the Jews. I'd be able to
do everything if I became President.*

*I would move Sing-Sing to Fifth
Avenue and I'd pretty up Allen
Street the way it used to be. I'd set
up the politician there, that's what
I'd work for. And to them all, every
last one, I'd affix the Union Label.
And all the policemen would get the
sack.*

*I'd quickly declare war, to go fight
the Russian and bury him deep in
the earth with the first blow. With
Japan, I'd teach him well this time.
And right after the battle I'd kill von
Plehve, the enemy of Israel. Then I'd
be very happy with the downfall of
the Russian bear*

Vyacheslav von Plehve

Oj, wus ch'bob gewolt. אי, וואם כ'האב געוואלם

Oi, wus ch'ob ge wolt, hob ich ois ge - führt, . .

Sol ich a -soi leben Ch'hob ge wolt a schön Jün-ge le,

Hot mir Got ge ge ben Ch'hob ge maint as er is schoin main,

Ch'hob ihm schoin ba - ki - men; Is ge - kü - men-a

schö ner Mei- de -le Ün hot ihm zü -ge - nü -men.

וױ אזױ קען איך לוסטיג זײן,
אז פֿארשטערט זענען מיר מײנע וועגען?
אז איך דערמאָן מיך אָן זײן שעהן פנים,
וױ אזױ קאָן איך לעבען?

איך עם און טרינק און שלאָף בײ נאכט,
נאָר מײן הארץ איז מיר פֿארטראכט.
וױ אזױ קען איך לוסטיג זײן,
אז פֿארשטערט זענען מיר מײנע וועגען?
אז איך דערמאָן מיך אָן זײן שעהן פנים,
וױ אזױ קען איך לעבען?

(וואַרשא)

139

I sought this one at the request of a reader., who sent me an Aaron Lebedeff recording. The verse as Lebedeff sang it was a version of the folksong printed in Warsaw (see left). He added a chorus. He sent the song to the US Copyright Office - designated a "duo" and combined with other melodic material. Aaron Lebedeff probably improvised verses to some extent and so in my version on page 142 I wrote my own verses.

Duet – Vus Ich Hob Gevalt

Vos kh'hob gevolt hob ikh oysgefirt

Vos kh'hob ge volt hob ikh oys-ge-firt zol ikh a-zoy leb - n kh'hob ge-volt a maz-l fayn, hot es mir Got ge

geb - n ay ay   ay ay   ay ay ay ay voyl vi di velt

shves-ter horkht mir: halt zikh fray, tantst vi di tsi - gan-kes vayl zor-ge-nish un du-le-nish es

helft vi a toyt n ban-kes ay ay   ay ay   ay ay ay ay voyl vi di velt

Dm
Ikh hob gehat a nomen far a gliklekhe bas mazl
E   Dm   Gm
Nor glik iz rund, es geyt avek, itst betl ikh un gazl

Dm
Vos toyg mir aylenish un bren? Vos toyg mir gikh tsu yogn?
E   Dm   Gm
Es toyg mir beser yedn tog gute shpayzn in dem mogn

Dm
Avade, es gefelt mir zeyer a hering mit patates
E   Dm   Gm
Nor khap a hering a mol on gelt un zits zikh hinter krates

Dm
Avek mit tsores on a shir mit umru un mishlakhes (calamity)
E   Dm   Gm
Avek mit more-shkhoyre! Ikh vel hobn bald fil nakhes

Dm
Dem beyzer vil ikh ibermakhn, dem tsar vel ikh bazign
E   Dm   Gm
Tsu hobn fraynt un a varem hoyz s'iz a genugik fargenign

What I wanted, I succeeded in, let me go on that way. I wanted good luck and God gave it to me. Sisters, listen: Stay free, dance like the gypsies Because worry and bother, they help like a bandaid on a corpse. I used to be considered a lucky girl But luck is round, it rolls away. Now I beg and steal. What good is hurrying to me? What good is it to rush around? I'd rather just have good food in my belly every day

Naturally, I love herring with potatoes, But just grab a herring once without paying for it, You'll sit behind bars. I'm going to transform and vanquish indignation and rage Friends and a warm house: that's enough pleasure for me. Away with endless trouble, with unrest and calamity Away with melancholy, I'll soon be joyful.

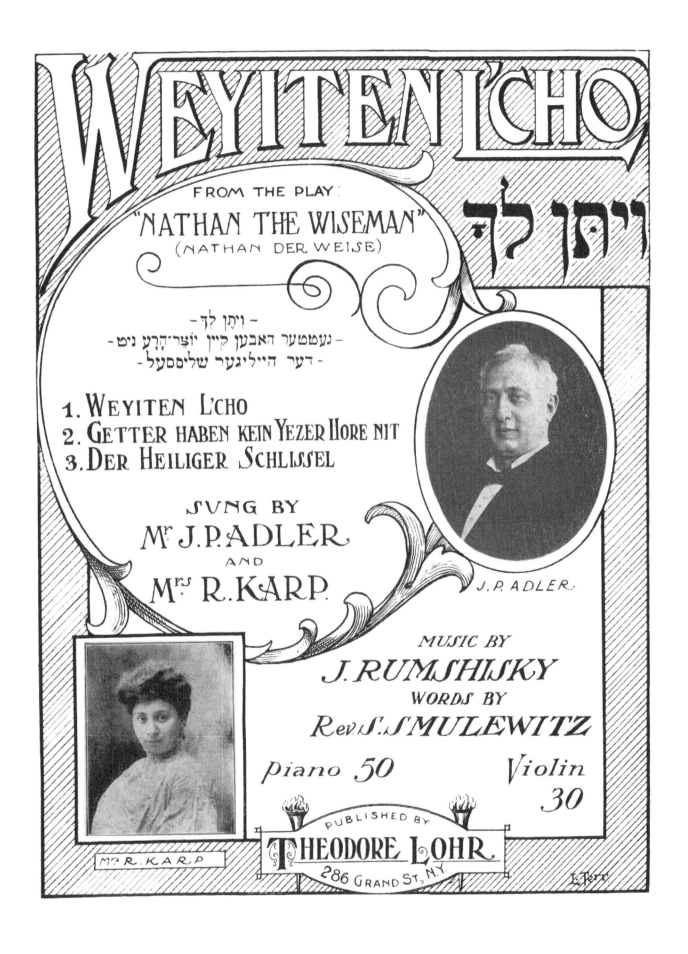

WEYITEN L'CHO

ויתן לך

FROM THE PLAY:
"NATHAN THE WISEMAN"
(NATHAN DER WEISE)

‐ וִיְתֶן לָך ‐
‐ געטטער האבען קיין יוֹצֶר‐הָרָע ניט ‐
‐ דער הייליגער שליסטעל ‐

1. WEYITEN L'CHO
2. GETTER HABEN KEIN YEZER HORE NIT
3. DER HEILIGER SCHLISSEL

SUNG BY
Mr J. P. ADLER
AND
Mrs R. KARP

J. P. ADLER

Mrs R. KARP

MUSIC BY
J. RUMSHISKY
WORDS BY
Rev. S. SMULEWITZ

Piano 50   Violin 30

PUBLISHED BY
THEODORE LOHR
286 GRAND ST. N.Y.

L. Terr

143

Wejiten l'cho.

144

wil-len gro-ser herr kein kinder nit sein mehr menshen gro-se sein is un-ser zweck far

sich a bal-le boss in gibste uns et-wos nem-es Got-te niu nit a week Ja We-

CHORUS.
Moderato.

Ji ten le cho mi tal ha sho ma-yim Jitz choks-bro che sei got me ka-yim

fel der wel der frucht in wein sol beim yü den to mid sein

mach die son im far uns sich kni en mach sei got te niu zu-shand

Wejiten 1,cho 3

in Je - ru sho la jin Zi - on sol sein un ser fa - ter land. *f*

We are, oh! dear God, after all,
Your children. And precisely because of that, we suffer,
you treat us like small children.
You play with our feelings, you give us an exquisite land,
It's just a plaything to play with, and soon you take it back.
We want, dear God, to be children no longer.
It's our goal to be grown up people, our own masters,
And you give us something, God, don't take it away, oy vey,

"And he gives heaven and earth"
Fulfill the blessing of Isaac!
Forests, fields, fruit and wine, may Jews always have them,
Make our enemies bow before us, God, bring them to disgrace,
And Jerusalem - Zion, shall be our fatherland.

We have great faith in you
We know you're not mocking us.
Fulfill what you promised to our holy generations,
You said your people Israel would multiply like the stars
But of course what's multiplying is our tears
Stones rain down on us without end,
Dear God, we want no more stones!

צוויי חזנים
TWO CANTORS

COMEDY BY
KALMANOVITZ

ADAPTED BY
B. THOMASHEFSKY

MUSIC BY
HERMAN WOHL

WORDS BY
B. THOMASHEFSKY

"SISU VESIMCHU" SUNG BY DAVID KESSLER

"YEDER EINER STREIKT ATZIND" SUNG BY SAM KASTEN

LYRIC BY L. GILROD

Published by HARRY THOMASHEFSKY
THOMASHEFSKY THEATRE
NEW YORK

PHONOGRAPH RECORDS
OF "TWO CANTORS"
WILL BE ISSUED ~~~~
SHORTLY BY
THOMASHEFSKY RECORD CO.

Yeder eyner straykt atsind

Louis Gilrod

Herman Wohl, 1919

Ni - shto haynt mer keyn pay - kers haynt ze - nen a - le

stray - kers di shnay - ders un di shus - ters un di be - kers stray - ken itst. Di kars, di e - le -

ve - ters di ek - ters in the - a - ters di kon - duk - tors in di sob - veys un der oy - lem un - ter

shtitst. Ir kumt a - rayn in res - to - rant far - hun - gert zey - er mat a steyk mit frayt pe - ti - tis or - dert

ir baym vey - ter shnel. baym ersh - tn bis der - zet ir fis fun a vo - king de - li - gat er zogt eyn vort un

a - le vey - ters stray - ken af der shtel. Der vey - ter makht keyn shtik nemt tsu dem steyk tsu - rik.

Ye - der ey - ner shrayt a - tsind leb - n zol di zi - se tsayt. Ye - der ey - ner zogt a - tsind

leb - n zoln di u - nion layt. Oy, bri - der - lekh_ s'iz git mar - shirt, hot keyn moy - re nit

Van - der - bilt - n shteyt a - roys a fayg, a fayg. Hur - ray far Ka - rl Marks. di

bos - ses ze - nen in der baks di u - nion layt ge - vi - nen yed - n strayk, yedn strayk!

Nishto haynt mer keyn paykers. Haynt zenen ale straykers!
Di shnayders un di shusters un di bekers strayken itst.
Di kars, di eleveters, di ekters in theaters,
Di konduktors in di sobveys un der oylem untershtitst.

Ir kumt arayn in restorant farhungert zeyer mat.
A steyk mit frayt petitis ordert ir baym veyter shnel.
Baym ershtn bis derzet ir fis fun a voking deligat.
Er zogt eyn vort un ale veyters strayken af der shtel.

Der veyter makht keyn shtik, nemt tsu dem steyk tsurik.

Yeder eyner shrayt atsind lebn zol di zise tsayt.
Yeder eyner zogt atsind lebn zoln di union layt.
Oy, briderlekh s'iz git! Marshirt, hot keyn moyre nit!
Vanderbiltn shteyt aroys a fayg, a fayg.
Hurray far Karl Marks. Di bosses zenen in der baks
Di union layt gevinen yedn strayk, yedn strayk!

These days there are no more shirkers. Everyone is a striker.
The tailors, the shoemakers, and the bakers are striking now.
The streetcars, the elevators, the actors in theaters,
The subway conductors ... and people support them.

You come into a restaurant hungry and tired,
You quickly order a steak with potatoes from the waiter.
As you take the first bite you see the feet of a walking delegate.
He says one word and all the waiters strike right away.

The waiter doesn't fool around, he takes your steak away.

Everyone is striking now, long live the sweet time.
Everyone is striking now, long live the union members.
Oh, brothers, it's good! March, don't be afraid!
Give Vanderbilt the finger.
Hurray for Karl Marx! The bosses are cornered.
The union members win every strike!

Yente di Royte

They propose to marry me to a fool - red-headed Yente Red-headed Yente: a beautiful girl, just like gold. Oh how beautiful her face is, a dot of charm, She has no teeth in her mouth It's an emergency! I'm a fugitive! I'm running from red-headed Yente like I'd run from death

Red-headed Yente has a wooden leg and a glass eye Leathery hands, a pointy nose, that's red-headed Yente Oh how sweet, with her crooked legs, The gal's a giant, she's an ugly woman It's an emergency! I'm a fugitive! I'm running from red-headed Yente like I'd run from death

"I don't want him, that hypocrite," said red-headed Yente "What a parasite, a bandit!" said Yente the red-headed girl "Ugh, how awful, what a piker, He's revolting at night, he doesn't know what should be done Somebody should slap him! I laugh at that bungler." says Yente the red-headed girl.

Me redt mir a shidekh, nit keyn yold, mit Yente di
Royte
A sheyne moyd, vi der toyt iz Yente di Royte Moyd
Okh, vi zis, zenen ire krume fis
Ven zi geyt un shmuest, genetst un hist

Ikh bin far noyt antloyfn vi fun a toyt
Fun Yente di Royte Moyd

Tut keyn zakh, nor zi redt...
Zi libt tsu shlofn biz tsvelf in bet...
Okh vi sheyn ir volt zi nor gezen
A pintele mit kheyn in moyl hot zi keyn tseyn

A shpitsikn shtern mit a lange noz hot...
Arayngemakht tseyn un eyn oyg fun gloz hot...
Okh, a shpas hob ikh gehat in gas
Vayl zi iz grob vi a fas - a noz vi a bas

Lign zogn plotkes trogn kon ...
Zukhn by di tashn fun di teplekh nashn...
Derzen hob ikh di zekste make af ir kop
Fet vi a krop mit a tsugezetste tsop

They made me a match, no chump, with Red Yente
A girl pretty as death is Red Yente
Oh how sweet are her crooked feet
When she walks and talks, yawns and sneezes

It was an emergency, I ran from her as from a
corpse from Red Yente

She does nothing but talk
She loves to sleep in bed till noon
Oh, how beautiful she is, just look
Her charms... she has no teeth...

Red Yente has a pointed forehead and a long nose
Crooked teeth and a glass eye
Oh, I had a joke in the street
Because she's fat as a barrel

Red Yente can tell lies and carry fish
She can pickpocket and snack from the pots
I saw the sixth plague on her head
Fat as a plump chicken, with a braid

יענטע די רויטע מויד .

1.

מען רעדט מיר אַ שידוך, ניט קיין יאָלד
מיט יענטע די רויטע...
אַ שעהנע מויד – וי דער טויט
איז יענטע די רויטע מויד.
אַך, וי זיס – זענען איהרע קרומע פיס
ווען זי געהט און שמועסט, גענעצט און היסט.
איך בין פאַר נויט – אַנטלאָפען וי פון אַ טויט. ‏בים.
פון יענטע די רויטע, יענטע די רויטע, יענטע די
רויטע מויד.

2.

זי טהוט קיין זאך נאָר זי רעדט
יענטע די רויטע...
זי ליעבט צו שלאָפען ביז 12 אין בעט
יענטע די רויטע מויד.
אַך, וי שעהן – איהר וואָלט זי נאָר געזעהן
אַ פינטעלע מיט עפּ חן – אין מויל האָט זי קיין ציהן.
איך בין פאַר נויט – אַנטלאָפען וי פון אַ טויט. ‏בים.
פון יענטע די רויטע, יענטע די רויטע, יענטע די
רויטע מויד.

3.

אַ שפּיציגען שטערען מיט אַ לאַנגע נאָז
האָט יענטע די רויטע...
אַריינגעמאַכטע ציהן און איין אויג פון גלאָז
האָט יענטע די רויטע מויד.
אַך, אַ שפּאַס – האָב איך געהאַט אין גאַס
ווייל זי איז גראָב וי אַ פאַס – אַ נאָז וי אַ באַס. ‏בים.
איך בין פאַר נויט – אַנטלאָפען וי פון אַ טויט.
פון יענטע די רויטע, יענטע די רויטע, יענטע די
רויטע מויד.

4.

ליגען זאָגען – פלאָטקעס טראָגען
קאָן יענטע די רויטע...
זוכען ביי די טאַשען – פון די טעפּלעך נאַשע,
קאָן יענטע די רויטע מויד.
דערזעהן האָב איך – די 6טע מכּה אויף איהר קאָפּ,
פעט וי אַ קראָפּ – מיט אַ צוגעזעצטען צאָפּ.
איך בין פאַר נויט – אַנטלאָפען וי פון אַ טויט. ‏בים.
פון יענטע די רויטע, יענטע די רויטע, יענטע די
רויטע מויד.

152

Yidishe Kazatzke

Joseph Rumshinsky 1920

Za - i - grai - tye mnye Ko - za tshok po mis - nagd - ski po - kha - sid - ski hop hop hop Vos men meg, meg men mit dem reb - ns koyekh vos men tor - nit meg men oykh. Oy! Gdal - ti u ge - boyr - ti eyn le sa - per a pe - ri - kl mish - na - yes iz af al - es me - kha - per vot te - bye vot te - bye ko - za - tshok, po mis - nagd - ski po kha - sid - ski hop hop hop Okh! yis - me - khu b - mal - khus kho shom - rey sha - bes oy vey oy vey sha - bes oy vey oy vey sha - bes vot te - bye ko - za - tshok vot te - bye ko - za - tshok oy vey oy vey sha - bes oy oy oy bes oy oy

Play me a kazachok Misnaged-style, Chasidic-style
What one may do, one does with the rebbe's strength
What is forbidden, one can do that also.
Oy, I grew up and I grew strong, impossible to recount.
A little chapter of mishnah atones for everything.
There's a kazachok for you! Misnaged-style, Chasidic-style
Those who observe Shabbat and call it a delight...
Oy vey, Shabbat. There's a kazachok for you!
Oy vey, Shabbat.

THE WAR OF WEALTH

JACOB LITT
PROPRIETOR

C.T. DAZEY
Author of
IN OLD KENTUCKY

THE RUN ON THE BANK A CRISIS IN THE AFFAIRS OF THE GREAT FINANCIAL INSTITUTION. THE MOST ANIMATED & REALISTIC SCENE EVER SHOWN ON THE STAGE.

Miss NELIE KASSMAN

THE "NEW TRANS-ATLANTIC HEBREW LINE"

FOR THE EXCLUSIVE USE OF "THE PERSECUTED."

Di zibn boarders

Solomon Small

Mayn ersh-ter boar-der Ro-sen er flegt zikh to-mid blo-zn far dray dol-lar te mit kof-fe va-shn vesh un haynt fun so-fe ayn-ge-bro-khn bor-ekh ha-shem dem spring ge-ven a groy-ser na-sher far im nit veyk nit ka-sher kri-khn flegt er in di tep-lekh kh'zol im makh-n khrem-slekh krep-lekh s'hot zikh im ge-gen-zlt a-les ding Hert zikh vayb-lekh ayn leygt nor tsu dem kop nemt fun mir a mu-ser zikh a-rop vilt ir leb-n fayn der kop zol ru-ik zayn lost in hoyz keyn bor-der nit a-rayn.

Mayn tsvey-ter boar-der Kra-ser, a yi-di-sher far-fa-ser Flegt er shray-bn flegt er mek-n s'flegt a gan-tsn tog mir klek-n Blay-bn-dik in

156

Mayn ershter boarder Rosen er flegt zikh tomid blozn.
Far dray dollar te mit koffe vashn vesh un haynt fun sofe
Ayngebrokhn borkh hashem dem spring
Geven a groyser nasher far im nit veyk nit kasher
Krikhn flegt er in di teplekh kh'zol im makhn khremslekh kreplekh
s'hot zikh im gegenzlt ales ding

Hert zikh vayblekh ayn leygt nor tsu dem kop, nemt fun mir a muser zikh arop
vilt ir lebn fayn der kop zol ruik zayn - lost in hoyz keyn border nit arayn.

Mayn tsveyter boarder Kraser, a yidisher farfaser,
Flegt er shraybn, flegt er mekn, s'flegt a gantsn tog mir klekn
Blaybendik in shtub mit im aleyn
Flegt mir makhn zitsn, hern zayne skitsn,
Forgeshtelt mir lebns-bilder! Eynmol hot mayn man der vilder
Oysgezetst fun moyl im ale tseyn!

Mayn driter boarder Breyver, s'mazl im in keyver...
Hot dem gantsn front farnumen ven mayn man flegt dortn kumen,
Hot er shoyn dos laydn nit gevolt
Flegt zikh mit mir shafn vi mit zayns a shklafn
Zikh gehaltn far a makher, iz geven a dever-akher
Rent far dray monatn nit batsolt!

Mayn ferter boarder Traybl hot gehat a vaybl
Flegt zi kumen shrayen, sheltn, Zidln undz un kern veltn
Vos mir hobn ir ir glik geroybt
Aza min kalakotke ongemakht a plotke
Hot mayn man farshteyn gegebn az der boarder iz mayn lebn
Un mayn groyser khokhem hot gegloybt!

Mayn finfter boarder Beygl a khevre-man, a foygl
Er hot fun mayn erlekh hayzl gor gemakht a gembling klayzl
Kortn-shpiler hobn nit gefelt!
Kh'hob gehat fun "Pinke" un nokh fun zakhn linke
Eyn fartog iz er farshvundn, hobn zol er tsores, vundn,
Oysgeramt mayn 'jewelry' un gelt!

Mayn zekster boarder Spekter iz geven an ekter
Do hot mir mayn shlag getrofn biz nokh mitog flegt er shlofn
Kh'hob di hoyz nit oyframen gekent
Un ven er flegt dervakhn, flegt er probes makhn:
Veynen, shrayen, kvitshen, zingen
Mayne oyern farklingen, un mit "peses" opgetsolt zayn rent

Mayn letster boarder Reyner iz geven a sheyner
Hot farmogt a zisn shmeykhl un gehat a yam mit seykhl
Mir geakht, geshetst mayn yeder trit
Flegt zikh prost basmakn fun mayn kokhn, bakn
Nor nit lang iz er farblibn, S'hot mayn brokh im gor fartribn
Un mer keyn boarders haltn lozt er nit!

My first boarder, Rosen, was a blowhard. For three dollars, tea and coffee, I washed his clothes and on top of that: He broke the spring in my sofa. He was a big eater, for him no ? nothing kosher. He used to sneak into the booze... He wanted me to make him kremslekh and kreplekh. He had a hankering for everything.

Listen, women, get this in your heads, take advice from me. If you want to live well and peacefully Don't let any boarders into your house.

My second boarder, Kraser, was a Yiddish author. He used to write, he used to erase, He used to be after me all day to hang out in his room with him, alone. He used to make me sit and listen to his skits, He performed scenes from life for me. Once my wild husband knocked out all his teeth.

My third boarder Breyver, may he rest in peace, He used to ? be busy when my husband used to come in. He didn't want to suffer. He used to boss me around as if I were his slave He considered himself a bigshot, he was a pig/scoundrel! He didn't pay rent for three months!

My fourth boarder Traybl had a wife, she used to come shouting and cursing, Berating us and turning things upside down Because we'd robbed her of her happiness Such a chatterbox causing an uproar She implied to my husband the boarder was my love And my genius believed her!

My fifth boarder Beygl was a great guy, a sly one, He made of my respectable home a gambling house. Card players were not in short supply! I had money, and lots of dubiously legal stuff. One day he disappeared, may he have miseries and wounds, He stole my jewelry and money!

My sixth boarder, Spekter, was an actor. What a pest! He slept till past noon, I couldn't clean the house. And when he'd wake up, he used to rehearse: Crying, shouting, shrieking, singing, My ears were ringing. And he paid his rent with theater passes.

My last boarder Reyner was handsome, He had a sweet smile and was very smart. He esteemed me, he doted on my every step. He used to simple inhale my cooking, my baking, But he didn't stay for long... My disaster of a husband drove him out And wouldn't allow any more boarders.

For Yiddish books, songbooks, tunebooks, cds and more, see

http://yiddishemporium.com

or write jane@mappamundi.com

Made in the USA
Middletown, DE
28 October 2022

13699602R00091